My special thanks are due to my husband, Alan, for his skilful photography and to my friends who lent me containers and allowed me to cut from their gardens.

© Edith Brack 1988 text and photographs

ISBN 1 85648 104 2

This edition published 1992 by the Promotional Reprint Company Limited exclusively for Selecta Book Ltd, Folly Road, Roundway, Devizes, Wiltshire, SN10 2HR.

CONTENTS

INTRODUCTION

Most people need some means of creative expression to enhance their lives and for many thousands it is the fascination of flower arranging with its many facets which has filled the gap.

It is an art or craft—call it what you will—which, with only a moderate amount of study and expenditure, can enhance the attractiveness of your home and give you a satisfying sense of achievement.

Unlike the potter with an amorphous lump of clay, the wood carver with an uninspiring chunk of wood and the painter with a blank canvas, we have things of beauty to start with. The choice of flowers and foliage is infinite and with such splendid raw materials you are more than half-way there before you begin!

Flower arranging is not a difficult subject on which to embark, you can start with just a few easily obtainable tools and containers, some elementary tips and no more than a modicum of artistic talent. Anyone can quickly learn how to create an arrangement. Don't say, as so many people do: 'It's not for me, I'm not artistic.' Everyone is to some extent artistic—how else would we choose our clothes, our furnishings, our wallcoverings and paint?

This book is designed to set you on the right path to becoming a flower arranger. It begins with the tools of the trade which includes all the basic essentials for starting off. The guidelines on design deal with the accepted principles and elements of design which are the basis of any art form. All the basic shapes and styles of arranging and techniques are discussed and illustrated as these represent the building-blocks for all your designs and the more advanced aspects are also considered in detail. Finally, as the twenty-first century draws near The Way Ahead suggests a more adventurous and creative approach.

Even though you are a traditionalist at heart it is well worth having an open mind and exploring the modern way of arranging—how else can you be considered *the complete flower arranger*?

1

making a Start

PART ONE Tools of the Trade

Most homes already possess the basic equipment needed to start flower arranging like scissors, secateurs, buckets and a sharp knife but there are a few more extras you may have to purchase as your skills progress.

BASIC ESSENTIALS

Scissors

Florist's stub scissors are excellent as they are sharp, light and easy to handle. They not only cut stems but wire as well. Some prefer the larger and heavier Japanese style of cutters but these take more practice to use successfully.

Secateurs

A good pair of secateurs is essential for cutting much thicker branches and woody stems. It is worth purchasing a lightweight pair especially for your flower arranging as the average garden types are much heavier and cumbersome to carry about.

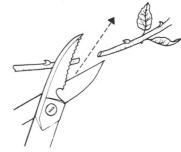

Knife

Choose a sharp lightweight knife with a reasonably long blade as it will be used for cutting floral foam as well as scraping stems.

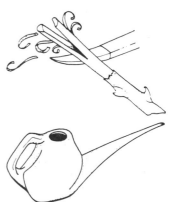

Watering can

Choose the type of can which has a long spout primarily designed for watering pot-plants and one that will hold at least a pint of water.

Spray
A small misting spray is a boon for keeping arrangements in tip-top condition.

Buckets
Special deep flower buckets with side handles for easy lifting are a good investment but failing this an ordinary household bucket, preferably with the handle removed, will suffice.

Polythene sheeting and bags
Plastic sheeting is useful for covering surfaces and plastic bags for carrying wet floral foam or plant material.

Wire cutters
They are a useful addition to your basic equipment for cutting wire which is too tough for your stub scissors.

Stem strippers
A stem stripper shaped like serrated-edged sugar tongs is another useful gadget. Pressed together and drawn down the flower stems, it will remove thorns or leaves quickly.

MECHANICS

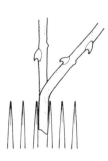

Flower arrangers in general refer to all equipment required for holding their plant materials in position as 'mechanics'. All these items can be purchased at florists' shops, garden centres or at horticultural shows.

Pinholders
Pinholders are made with a heavy lead base embedded with sharp vertical pins for impaling your plant material upon. They are not cheap but good ones will last a lifetime. It is worth building up a collection of various shapes and sizes. A 'well' pinholder is another good buy. It is a small receptacle for water made of lead with vertical pins embedded into the base. It will hold much heavier plant material without toppling over. Always remember to make a point of cleaning your pinholders

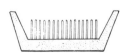

and straightening any of the pins which are bent before putting them away after use.

Use: It is always safer to fasten your pinholder to the base of your container with a green putty-like floral fixative sold specially for this purpose. If you should wish to use the pinholder in a tall container, first fill it to the required height with sand and then place the pinholder on the top. The stems of your plant material are then inserted on to or between the pins. Press them down vertically and then angle them from this position as you wish. When using a pinholder in a shallow container hide it from view with the strategic placement of pebbles or stones.

Wire netting

The use of wire netting has been largely superseded by floral foam but it is still an excellent and economic way of holding flowers in large containers. Sometimes called chicken wire it is usually sold in long rolls. However, a search round your local shops may produce a shopkeeper willing to sell it in short lengths. It is best to buy the 2in, 5cm mesh as you will find anything smaller will not accept the flower stems once inserted into the container.

Use: First remove the thick selvedge with your wire cutters. For a tall container cut a rectangle of netting the width of the container and three times its depth. Roll it into a loose sausage shape, bend it in half and push the U-bend into the bottom of the container leaving some of the loose ends standing proud above the container rim. These loose ends can be wrapped around the tall stems for extra support. The flower stems are then inserted at the desired angles in between the crumpled wire. Wire netting can also be used to cover the floral foam for extra security when doing a large arrangement. It can also help to secure heavy branches on a pinholder by crumpling a small piece, pressing it down on the pins and using the loose ends to wrap round the branch for extra support.

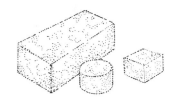

Floral foam

This green water-retaining plastic foam is sold in various shapes and sizes under a variety of trade names. Brick-sized blocks and small rounds are the most popular. It has revolutionized previous methods of flower arranging and made the once difficult task of placing plant material at angles a simple operation. There is a special foam for spring flowers and a non-porous variety for dried plant material.

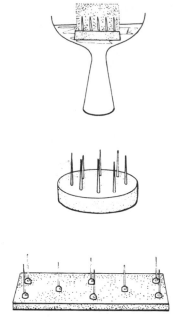

Use: Select a piece of foam with your container in mind. A round may be suitable, alternatively cut the required size and shape from a block. Soak it in a bowl of water until it sinks which means that it has absorbed all the water it can hold. When inserting the foam into a tall container make sure it stands proud above the rim of the receptacle and that there is ample room for topping up with water. With this in mind it is a good idea to place a square piece of foam in a round container and a round piece in a square container. If you are using a flat container your piece of foam should be secured to the base with either a 6-pronged lead or 4-pronged plastic holder specially made for the purpose. (If it is a large piece use more than one holder to be on the safe side.) As with the pinholder, make absolutely sure that the lead or plastic device is well secured to the base of the container with floral fixative. Most florists sell cheap green plastic dishes both round and oblong which are made especially for holding floral foam. This type of container is ideal for arranging flowers for someone in hospital or for a small thank-you gift when you don't expect the container to be returned.

Stub wires

A collection of wires in various gauges and lengths have many uses and can be obtained at florists' shops or garden centres.

Use: They can be used to straighten bent stems and for holding up heavy flower heads by carefully inserting a piece of strong wire up the stems to act as a splint. They can also be used for giving cones, seedheads and dried flowers false stems as well as supporting floppy leaves. In the latter case it is simply a matter of taping a piece of wire along the main rib of the leaf on the underside.

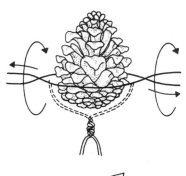

Reel wire

Fine silver binding wire and thicker gauge wire are both useful and can be bought on small reels.

Use: Mainly used for securing various items together such as chicken wire to the rim or handles of a container.

Cocktail or barbecue sticks

Both these items are used for holding fruit and vegetables in position in an arrangement.

Use: By inserting a cocktail stick half-way into one piece of fruit, leaving the other half free to insert into an adjoining piece, fruit can be held securely in an arrangement without

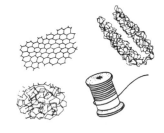

damaging it. For larger fruit and vegetables use the longer, stronger barbecue sticks. Larger fruit or vegetables can be safely lifted up in your designs for special effects by impaling them on a tripod of these sticks.

Candlecups

These are small containers in metal or plastic with a small protruberance in the base which fits snugly into the tops of candlesticks and candelabra.

Use: They enable you to display flowers in candlesticks, bottles and narrow-necked containers.

Candleholders

Small metal or plastic holders with spiked ends for holding candles in an arrangement.

Use: These holders will hold your candles securely upright when pressed into floral foam. An easy alternative can be made by taping 3 cocktail sticks equidistant around the base of a candle.

Florist's tape, Sellotape and elastic bands

All useful items.

Use: In various ways to make doubly sure of the stability of your mechanics.

Cones and tubes

They are made of metal or plastic and provide a means of raising up short-stemmed flowers in an arrangement.

Use: Attach a cone to a cane with silver wire or adhesive tape and insert either wire netting or foam inside, to hold the plant material in place. When the whole device is inserted into the container particular attention must be paid to its concealment. Small orchid tubes are invaluable for inserting flowers in displays of fruit for the table and for Sellotaping to glass jugs, punch bowls and carafes, enabling you to adorn the outsides with a few flowers and trails of ivy for a party table.

Plasticine, floral fixative

For most people modern fixative has replaced Plasticine. If you have any difficulty removing it from precious containers, use cotton wool soaked in white spirit.

Use: Before using any fixative make sure that the surfaces are dry. Place three small blobs of fixative on the base of the pinholder or other object to be secured, press down and give a slight twist.

Lead

A small sheet of plumber's lead is a useful extra.

Use: Strips of lead can be used instead of wire for securing chicken wire in a container. It is also useful for securing heavy branches. Cut a strip 1in, 2.5cm wide and about 10in, 25cm long, cut down centre to half-way mark and open up into a Y-shape. Insert the trunk part into the floral foam or chicken wire and wrap the two arms around the branch. A short piece of lead piping hooked on to the back of a large container is a good safety device to stabilize a top-heavy arrangement. The lead may be cut with either tin snips or a junior hacksaw.

Wedges

A couple of small wooden, rubber or plastic wedges can be a boon on occasions.

Use: A couple of wedges can level a container when faced with a sloping ledge, as is often the case in churches, or for stabilizing a container which is in itself unsteady.

CONTAINERS

Vase is a term rarely used these days; any receptacle for plant material is called a container and they can range from an antique bronze urn to a plastic saucer. Most homes can usually provide a wide selection of suitable items—bowls, tureens, flat stoneware cooking and serving dishes, decanters, candlesticks, an old copper kettle or maybe a silver cake basket; in fact anything that can hold water or can be made to hold water. Most arrangers delight in seeking out new containers and you will develop an eye like a bird-watcher's for spotting the rare and unusual. Some hand-crafted items may be expensive but many veritable treasures can be picked up for a song at junk shops, white elephant stalls, jumble sales and, the latest phenomenon, the car boot sale.

In general, containers look best in neutral shades and earthy colours, black in particular seems to enhance all flowers. White is a difficult colour for a container as it can be too eye-catching, but it is ideal for arrangements where white flowers predominate, as at weddings. If you have a container of a pleasing shape but the wrong colour, try spraying it with aerosol paint. Car paints are ideal for this and the wide selection of colours available gives an enormous palette from which to choose. For unusual effects try spraying it one colour and highlighting with another. Black and silver paint mixed together gives an attractive pewter finish while brown and gold produces an interesting bronze. It's great fun experimenting with different mediums and oil paints, wood and floor stains, emulsion paints and even ordinary household gloss all have their uses.

For easy reference, here is a list of various types of containers to consider for your collection.

Alabaster
This is expensive to buy but a gem-like addition to your collection. Alabaster pieces are usually bowl or urn-shaped and delicately shaded in pastel tints of cream, fawn and pink. But be careful, water can ruin the surface of alabaster so be on the safe side and insert another container as a lining. Alabaster table lamps can be adapted to hold water by screwing on a universal candle-cup device in place of the lamp holder.

Baskets
The woven wicker varieties are inexpensive to buy and ideal for the less sophisticated style of arranging. They come in all shapes and sizes but usually need a receptacle of some kind for holding the water, although baskets can be purchased complete with metal linings. Small pottery baskets or silver cake baskets make delightful containers for more sophisticated designs.

Basketry
Other items include plant holders, cornucopias, trays and even miniature wickerwork furniture which can all be adapted for displaying flowers and fruit.

Brass
Bowls, boxes and trays add a certain lustre to your flower arrangements and can often be picked up reasonably cheaply in junk shops.

Bronze
Chinese and Japanese bronze urns and *usubatas* are the

ultimate choice but beyond most people's cash limits. Nevertheless, a more modest bronze urn on a marble base is a possibility. (Failing this see Spelter.)

Cast iron

Old pots, pans and kettles including modern reproductions from the Far East, like the well-buckets with their lovely pebbly texture, make excellent containers. The drawback with anything iron, of course, is that it will soon rust if water is left in it for any length of time. To overcome this fault try heavily waxing them on the inside.

Ceramics

This includes earthenware, china, stoneware and porcelain—so classified because of the differing degrees of heat at which the pieces are fired in the kiln and the various types of clay from which they are made. Stoneware is the toughest and porcelain the most fragile. Containers of all shapes and sizes are made in earthenware and stoneware and as a rule are of a chunkier nature ideal for the modern type of arranging when fewer flowers are used. On the other hand containers made from china such as urns and bowls are more in keeping with the traditional style. Many porcelain items are very precious and have to be handled with great care but nevertheless they make delightful containers and you may be lucky enough to find a Dresden china figure, or something similar, with its own small vase hidden behind to hold a dainty arrangement.

Copper

Kettles, jugs, jelly moulds, bowls, dishes, preserving pans and even bed-warmers have their uses. The glow of highly-polished copper is marvellous for lighting up any dark corner and the advent of the 'long-life' cleaner has made this easier.

Fibreglass

It is now possible to purchase excellent reproductions of old urns and plant containers made in this medium which at first glance look like the real thing until you pick them up. They are extremely light and need some form of ballast to keep them from toppling over.

Glass

Bowls, decanters and vases come in a wide variety of shapes, sizes and colours but the more brightly coloured are not really suitable for effectively displaying flowers. The one drawback with glass is that it is transparent and you have to find an acceptable way of arranging your flowers in them. Sometimes it is possible to fit a candlecup holder on the top of the container so that the stems will not show or you can make the stems part of the design. If the container has a narrow neck try arranging the flowers in your hand. When you are satisfied with the result secure the stems with a piece of wire. Alternatively you can use lead strip and hook this over the back of the container to hold the flowers in place. A strategically placed leaf will hide your mechanics, in these instances it is often a case of trial and error. I have seen a glass container filled with glass marbles where the stems of the flowers were threaded through them and they made an unusual and very effective means of support. When arranging in glass it must be clean and sparkling with no tell-tale stains showing. Sometimes it is difficult to remove stains from narrow necked vases and decanters and I have always found the old fashioned trick of adding broken eggshells to soapy water to be the answer.

Home-made containers

All kinds of fascinating containers can be easily made at home with a little ingenuity. Flat containers can be made from sheets of lead or waterproofed plaster of Paris; tall containers from drain pipes, tins and plastic bottles covered with split bamboo, string, DIY plaster filler, self-adhesive plastic covering, sheet pewter or copper. A compote can be made from three separate parts—a dish, a stem and a base joined together, covered with plaster filler and then painted. It is great fun to make containers especially when they are your original idea. If you get the opportunity to attend evening classes in pottery, seize it with both hands. You will have great fun making your own individual containers and accessories.

Marble

Old marble urns and bowls can still be found and imported modern Italian marble reproductions are available. Marble is more durable than alabaster and will hold water.

Ormolu

Compotes or tazzas for fruit, ornamental vases and candlesticks are the main items in this ware, which is an alloy of metals (tin, copper and brass) with either bronze or gilt finish.

Pewter

Mugs, tankards, pitchers, teapots, bowls, candlesticks, platters and plates all make splendid containers for flowers. Pewter looks attractive whether left dull or polished. To polish, mix some whiting powder with linseed oil, rub in well with a soft rag and polish off with chamois leather.

Plastic

Containers of all shapes and sizes are now made in plastic and if you wish they can easily be sprayed with aerosol car paints to make very acceptable containers. The obvious advantage is that they are light to carry about and less breakable than equivalent pottery containers.

Silver

Trays, epergnes, cake baskets, jugs, entrée dishes, wine coolers and even the old-fashioned trumpet vases can all be made to hold flowers. The problem with silver is that it will easily stain inside so if possible conceal another container of some kind to hold the flowers. Failing this, line the silver with thin plastic before adding your chosen mechanics. Silver must always be well-polished to look its best and 'long-term' silver foam is the answer. Any items which are not constantly in use should be stored in polythene bags to retain their shine.

Spelter

In the nineteenth century, as a cheap substitute for bronze, many figurines, candelabra, jugs and other decorative pieces were mass-produced by casting from zinc (or an alloy of zinc and lead) and given a bronze finish to resemble the real thing. This ware was known as spelter. Many of these figurines can be adapted to make elegant holders for flowers, as in most cases they were designed with one hand held aloft bearing a torch or other artefact. This can be removed and a candlecup holder soldered on in its place. Similarly you may find items which resemble pewter but which are of an imitative alloy called Britannia metal.

Wood

Most of the wooden items suitable for holding flowers have not been made for that purpose except for some bamboo containers from the Far East. To make sure bamboo containers do not 'sweat' swirl polyurethane varnish around the inside before bringing them into use. Wooden trugs, tea caddies, old salt and knife boxes, bowls and miniature wheel-barrows are some examples. Under this heading, of course, comes the flower arranger's special favourite—driftwood.

BASES

Bases have a number of uses. Their original purpose was to prevent scratch and water marks on furniture but they can also be employed to make a small container look more important or to unify a design where accessories have been included. Frequently a base is used as a matter of course when the design would really look better without it, so make sure you really need it by taking it away and seeing the result before you make your final decision.

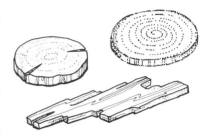

Bases
They can come in all shapes and sizes and in all manner of materials and it's a case of choosing the right type to enhance your particular style of arrangement. Your collection could include—fabric-covered boards in different shapes, sizes and colours, table mats, cane trays and platters, trivets and flat dishes made from different metals, slivers of wood, burl boards (polished slices of wood cut through a burl), bamboo rafts, tiles, bread and chopping boards, slabs of marble, alabaster, slate and stone, thick cork mats, shapes cut from acrylic or other suitable materials, Japanese wooden and metal scroll bases and antique stands.

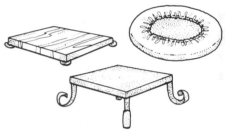

Pedestals
These are another type of base and although they can be used in the home they are usually brought into play for large free-standing arrangements for churches, exhibitions, shows and festive occasions.

You can buy pedestals made of wrought iron, alabaster, marble, fibreglass and carved wood or you can make your own quite easily. Here are a couple of ideas:

- Nail plywood on to a frame of battens and decorate with beading and plastic scrolls (the type sold for sticking on furniture at DIY shops) before painting with matt emulsion or aerosol paint.
- Take a compressed cardboard core (of the type used to support rolls of carpet, fabrics and plastic sheeting and often available from friendly shopkeepers) and add a

square or round base at the top and bottom by screwing on to either end of a piece of wood inserted into the centre of the core. Finally, paint or cover with imitation marble, self-adhesive plastic covering. The great advantage of these types of pedestal is that they are light and easy to transport and can soon be renovated if damaged.

PART TWO Tricks of the Trade

CONDITIONING OF PLANT MATERIAL

This term refers to the preparation of plant material to enable it to last as long as possible when cut. Garden foliage and flowers are best cut in the early morning or late evening. Take a bucket of water into the garden with you and place the stems in water *immediately*.

FOLIAGE

Branches
Strip off any unnecessary leaves from your branches, slit up the centre of the stem for about 2in, 5cm and place in deep water. The old-fashioned idea of hammering the ends of the stems has been proved to be detrimental as it encourages the growth of bacteria.

Young tender foliage which tends to droop quickly when cut can be given the 'boiling water treatment'. It sounds like a form of torture but it is quite harmless and helps the stems to take up water quickly. Hold the bottom inch, 2.5cm of the stem in boiling water for about 30 seconds, making sure that the leaves are protected from the steam by loosely wrapping with a cloth or greaseproof paper. Then place them in deep water.

Leaves
These respond best to total immersion overnight in a water

tank or even the bath. However, grey leaves must not be treated in this way because their velvety surfaces become waterlogged and spoil.

FLOWERS

Recut flower stems at a slant under water to prevent air-locks and then leave in deep water. Most bulb-grown spring flowers, however, are an exception to this rule. Because of the cellular structure of their stems they last better in shallow water.

Flowers with hollow stems
Flowers like delphiniums and lupins should have their hollow stems filled with water (a small funnel is ideal for this purpose) and plugged with a tiny piece of cotton-wool which will act as a wick to draw the water up the stem. Place in deep water. This treatment will have to be repeated if the stem is later recut.

Flowers with milky stems
Flowers like poppies and euphorbias exude a sticky white latex substance when cut. To prevent them bleeding further, singe the stem ends with a candle or gas flame and place in water. Repeat this treatment if stems have to be recut.

The 'boiling water treatment'
This procedure for cut foliage is equally beneficial for flowers. Hold the bottom inch, 2.5cm of stem in boiling water for about 30 seconds making sure the flowers are protected from the steam. This method is useful for florist's roses which have a tendency to hang their heads and for many other types of flowers such as dahlias, petunias, hellebores, hollyhocks, anemones, fuchsias, *Onopordums*, *Polygonums*, *Rudbeckias* and *Verbenas*. In fact, if you are having a problem with *any* type of flowers it is worth trying this treatment.

Submerging
If you completely submerge the stems and heads of clematis for about an hour, hydrangeas for a few hours and violets overnight it will greatly increase their lasting powers.

Bleach

Try adding some bleach to the water when conditioning gerberas to prevent them flopping. When arranging alliums a little bleach added to the water will remove any trace of smell.

Melted wax

This is used for keeping water lilies open. Pour the melted wax carefully between the petals.

Additives

There are a number of proprietary brands of powder on the market which can be added to the water to extend the life of flowers which I find helpful. Some people recommend sugar or an aspirin, others recommend standing flowers such as carnations in lemonade. It is another case of experimenting for yourself.

Misting spray

These sprays are usually sold for pot plants but they are excellent for keeping arrangements pristine especially in the warm atmosphere at shows and exhibitions.

Hair spray

Useful for 'setting' fluffy seedheads, grasses and bulrushes. Buy the cheapest brand.

De-thorning

To prevent damage to other flowers and foliage it is well worth removing the thorns from roses and other shrubs.

Wires

To make sure flowers like marigolds and zinnias do not hang their heads, carefully insert a wire up their hollow stems.

Florists' flowers

Inspect flowers carefully before purchasing and go for those which are just opening. They should have already been conditioned but recut the stems under water as soon as possible in case they have callused over.

2

Guidelines on Design

PRINCIPLES OF DESIGN

All art depends on certain principles and flower arrangement is no exception. There are no short cuts. But once an understanding of these basic principles has been fully assimilated into the subconscious, the arranger will find that she will be instinctively guided by them in all her work, without being aware of it.

Design is the planned relationship between all the component parts of any composition. To qualify as an acceptable design, an arrangement must first possess unity, scale, accent and, secondly balance, contrast, harmony and rhythm. Let us consider each in this order.

Unity

This means that no matter how many or few materials make up your composition or exhibit, flowers, foliage, container, base and any accessories must blend together harmoniously to make a unified whole.

Scale and proportion

This is the stumbling block for most beginners. It means the relationship in size between one component part of your design and another. Not only should you consider the size in relation of flowers to foliage, but also in relation to the size of the container, its base and any accessories you may wish to include. Scale, too, should be a consideration when placing an arrangement in a room for decoration and at shows when the size of your exhibit should be in scale with the space allowed for staging. A keen sense of size relationship is an asset to any arranger.

Accent and dominance

This is the means of directing the viewer's eye around your arrangement. It may be accomplished by utilizing shapes and sizes, colour, texture, contrast or repetition and even quantity. In most designs the eye is constantly drawn to the centre of interest or focal point but it should never be as obvious as the bull's eye on a dartboard.

Balance

'Visual' rather than 'actual' defines balance for the flower arranger. Even if an arrangement is quite stable it does not necessarily mean that the visual balance is correct. Does it look right? That is what you must ask yourself. To achieve balance the plant material should be so placed that there *appears to be* a similar amount on either side of an imaginary line running vertically through the centre of the arrangement. There are two types of balance—*symmetrical* where one side of the arrangement corresponds with the other and *asymmetrical* where the visual weight on either side is equal but the placements are dissimilar. In general an arrangement with asymmetrical balance is likely to be much more pleasing to the eye as it affords more opportunity for originality than one with symmetrical balance.

Good horizontal balance should also be assessed by imagining a line running across the centre of your arrangement. In this way you will be able to decide whether your arrangement is top or bottom heavy and if so it will enable you to make the necessary adjustments. Sometimes you will achieve balance by placement. This is when the plant material in an arrangement appears to be unbalanced in the container as in 'windswept' designs and the equilibrium can usually be restored by repositioning it in its setting. Look at the plant material and the container *as a whole* and judge its visual balance, taking into account the situation in which it is placed. For example, an arrangement which sweeps to the right should be placed on the left of the table and not in the centre so that counterbalance is achieved.

In any visual art the eyes may play tricks on us. Dark coloured flowers or foliage always appear heavier than similar light coloured materials, which is why they are used at the centre of an arrangement to give stability.

Contrast

This adds vitality as well as interest to an arrangement and can be achieved by the use of colour, texture, form and line.

However, it would be difficult to make an arrangement without contrasts since many plant materials are contrasting in themselves and care should be taken not to overdo this aspect of designing.

Harmony
Dealing with the aesthetic qualities of an arrangement rather than its physical properties, it is the acceptability of one part with another—the feeling that everything is just so. We could not accept daffodils with chrysanthemums nor could we accept coarse textured flowers and foliage in an elegant silver epergne. Personal preferences differ widely but there is a general consensus of opinion regarding the limits of acceptability.

Rhythm
The sense of movement which flows through an arrangement, achieved by repetition of lines, shapes and colours is rhythm. Its purpose is to create the impression of motion even though the plant material is static. At its best it can add distinction to an arrangement and make the ordinary into the extraordinary.

ELEMENTS OF DESIGN

Now that we have some idea of what constitutes the principles of design and some of the qualities a good arrangement must possess, let us now consider the elements of design. They consist of form, line, space, texture and colour.

Form
The term refers to the overall shape of any composition. It also applies to the individual parts which are used in constructing the whole. Form in plant material is divided into three basic shapes—rounds (termed 'points' in design language), lines and in-between (or transitional) shapes. Any plant material which is spherical is called a point, such as roses, daisies and chrysanthemums. Examples of 'line' plant material are spikes like iris leaves, gladioli and delphiniums. Transitional materials are those which reduce the contrast between the two. Leaves such as *Hostas*, *Bergenias* and other foliage along with half-open flowers fall into this group and are often referred to as 'fillers'.

Line

In contrast to form, line is the element which leads the eye from one part of the arrangement to the next in either a continuous or interrupted sequence.

Space

This refers to the voids between form and line, employed in the design of an arrangement. It should be noted that areas of enclosed space are equally important as form itself. Space surrounding an arrangement is vital to its presentation but this is usually dictated by the room elements where the arrangement is to be situated or, in the case of shows, by the size of niche alloted for your exhibit.

Texture

The visual and tactile qualities of any object is texture—it can be rough or smooth, shiny or dull, and fine or coarse. In staging an exhibit consideration should be given to the various textures of all the component parts and not the plant material alone. Just as various textures can harmonize with each other, different surfaces can also be used for contrast to avoid monotony in your design. The skilful use of texture can add enormously to the originality of an arrangement, especially in monochromatic designs.

COLOUR

Colour perhaps more than anything else causes the over-riding emotional response we get when viewing a flower arrangement. However well an arrangement is composed, bearing in mind all the principles and elements of design already discussed, it cannot reach perfection if the colour element is lacking in any way. The power of colour should not be underestimated, so it is important to know how the theory of colour works in relation to flower arranging.

Colour like sound is not a physical identity. It is merely a visual sensation. What we experience as colour is the effect of light rays being transmitted through the eye to the brain. If a beam of light is refracted through a prism it can be spread into a spectrum. Each part of the spectrum corresponds to a particular wavelength—the long-wave end produces red radiations and at the short-wave end we have the violet colours, in between are the orange, yellow, green and blue hues. Purples are a mixture of radiations from the two ends of the spectrum. Every schoolchild learns the colours of the rainbow and so the sequence of red, orange, yellow, green, blue and violet are instilled into our minds at an early age. These hues of the spectrum are usually displayed in the form of a ring known as the colour circle or wheel.

THE COLOUR CIRCLE *See page 24*

The outer band of the circle shows the pure colours or **hues**—red, orange, yellow, green, blue and violet. These are termed the **primary hues**. The division in between, such as red–orange and red–violet are called **secondary hues**. *Band 2* shows the **tints** derived from the outer band hue when white has been added. *Band 3* shows **tones** derived from the outer band of hue when grey has been added (a combination of black and white). *Band 4* shows the **shades** derived from the outer band hue when black has been added.

There is an infinite range of tints, tones and shades which can be derived from any different hue, but for the purpose of this colour circle only one of each is shown.

Although we speak of white and black as colours there are no such hues in the colour circle. White is the combination of all the prismatic hues and black the absence of all. When we speak of black, white and grey we speak of neutral or achromatic colours. For explanation of the dimensions of colour, hue, value and chroma, see chart overleaf.

Basic colour schemes or harmonies
There are two basic types of harmonies—those which appear side by side on the colour circle and those which are opposites. The former are referred to as 'related' and the latter as 'contrasted' harmonies.

Related harmonies are divided into two types:

Monochromatic harmonies are made up of variations of tints, tones and shades of a single hue. There may be variation of chroma best effected by using flower, foliage and accessories of different textures, but care should be taken not to stray either to the left or right on the colour circle.

Monochromatic colour schemes can produce stunning

A Flower Arranger's Guide to Colour Theory

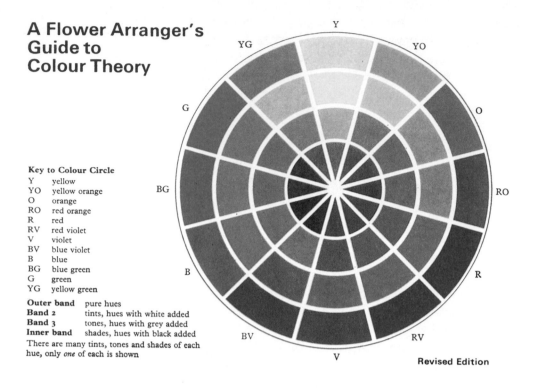

Revised Edition

Key to Colour Circle

Y	yellow
YO	yellow orange
O	orange
RO	red orange
R	red
RV	red violet
V	violet
BV	blue violet
B	blue
BG	blue green
G	green
YG	yellow green

Outer band   pure hues
Band 2   tints, hues with white added
Band 3   tones, hues with grey added
Inner band   shades, hues with black added
There are many tints, tones and shades of each hue, only *one* of each is shown

The Dimensions of Colour

Hue   refers to one colour as distinct from another, e.g. red as distinct from green

Value   refers to the lightness or darkness of a colour, the modification shown in tints, tones and shades of a hue

Chroma   refers to the amount of pure hue present in a colour, the strength or weakness of a colour

The term 'tone' is generally used for any colour deviating from a pure colour

Neutrals   Black, white and grey, also called achromatic colours

Basic Colour Schemes

Monochromatic   The use of tints, tones and shades of one colour
Analogous (Adjacent)   The use of 2–4 colours lying next to each other on the colour circle
Complementary   The use of colours which lie opposite or approximately opposite each other on the colour circle
Triadic   The use of three colours equidistant apart
Polychromatic   The use of many colours together

The diagrams below illustrate the principles of scheme selection

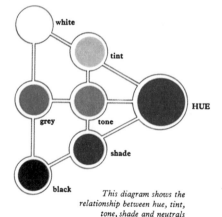

This diagram shows the relationship between hue, tint, tone, shade and neutrals

Monochromatic

Adjacent

Complementary

Triadic

designs. However, great care has to be taken with the selection of your plant material to make sure that every part of it falls within the tints, tones and shades of the single hue.

Analogous harmonies can include two, three or four colours adjacent to each other on the colour circle but the beginner will find the use of two or three hues with their tints, tones and shades easier to cope with.

Contrasting harmonies include:

Direct complementary harmony in which two hues directly opposite on the colour circle are used together, and/or their tints, tones and shades.

Near complementary—any hue, with either (but not both) of the two hues adjacent to its complement, for example yellow, and either blue—violet or red—violet.

Split complementary—a hue on one side of the colour circle, combined not with its direct opposite but with one on each side of it, for example red, plus yellow—green and blue—green but not green itself. There are also *double split complementary*, and *paired complementary*, *adjacent* and *analogous complements* but these complex schemes are rarely called for.

Triadic—the combination of three hues that are equidistant from each other on the colour circle, for example green, orange and violet.

Polychromatic—the use of many hues together. But take care, a multi-coloured scheme can be a hotchpotch unless great skill is shown in the blending of various hues.

These guidelines to various colour harmonies will give you an insight into the way colour can be effectively used in your arrangements. Where specific harmonies are called for at shows they should be strictly adhered to but arrangers should always be free to experiment and honour their own originality in other classes.

Psychological impact is another important factor in any discussion about colour and by this I mean the emotional response which colour evokes.

Warm and cool colours

When studying the colour circle we automatically divide it into two. Red, orange and yellow suggest warmth as they make us think of the sun and fire; they convey a feeling of cheerfulness, even excitement, although they can also suggest anger. Green, blue and violet on the other hand suggest coolness and quiet, peace and tranquillity, but they can also convey a feeling of depression and to some people even morbidness. It can be a fascinating exercise to write down all the colours and alongside them all the concept they convey to you, starting with red with its associations of anger, aggression, courage, danger, excitement, fire, friction, heat, love, martyrdom, strength and torture and so on working right through to violet.

Advancing and receding colours

Here again the same division of the colour circle applies. But this time we think of the warmer hues as advancing in character whilst the cool hues are retiring and receding.

Both these aspects of colour are especially useful when creating 'moods' for interpretative work at shows and exhibitions.

Colours, too, can appear light and heavy depending on their tonal values. Tints seem to have less weight than shades and so lighter coloured plant material is usually placed at the outer edges of arrangements and the darker shades towards the centre. Luminosity is another consideration when exhibiting. This is the quality that makes some colours stand out more than others in poor light. Therefore tints (a hue mixed with white) have a higher luminosity and can be used to advantage in dark environments.

You should always be aware of the type of lighting when you are displaying flowers as it can considerably alter colour. White fluorescent lighting turns reds into muddy browns, but it will enhance blue. Tungsten lighting (from domestic light bulbs) enhances reds, oranges and yellows but blues become dull and recede. For displaying blues and violets to their best advantage they should be seen in good daylight.

When considering the use of colour in flower arranging remember that it does not only refer to the flowers and foliage but to the container as well. Generally speaking, the choice of your container should be subservient to the colour scheme of your arrangement, but at the same time be aesthetically pleasing. Only in modern and abstract designs are violent colour contrasts used. Many people only associate particular colours with certain types of containers, for example pinks and mauves with silver, and oranges and reds with copper. Don't be over burdened with other peoples' opinions, use your own imagination and experiment with different colour combinations and you will surprise and delight yourself with your new ideas.

3 Basic Shapes of Arrangements

PART ONE
Geometrical Influence

SYMMETRICAL TRIANGLE   *See page 28*

Container
Marble urn

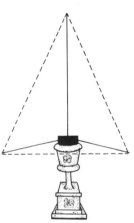

Mechanics
A small container has been inserted into the marble urn. This is fitted with a metal holder for securing the soaked floral foam which should stand proud above the rim of the container. Top up with water.

Plant material
Solidago 'Golden Mosa', Singapore orchids, spray carnations, roses, lilies, freesias, golden privet, *Hedera helix* 'Buttercup'

Method
Select suitable plant material for your outline. In this design the lemon spikes of the opening golden rod were selected to fit in with the chosen colour scheme. First insert the main vertical placement which should be about one and a half times the height of the container. The placements either side which define the triangular shape of your design should be a little shorter and inserted so that they come forward slightly to give depth to the arrangement. Next insert additional plant material to strengthen these lines. This is called 'transitional' or 'filler' material. Always try to keep these placements within an imaginary line drawn from the top to either side of the outline. They can be varied to give interest so try not to make one side a mirror image of the other. Remember, too, to place the plant material at different angles and on different planes

Above: Asymmetrical triangle
Left: Symmetrical triangle

otherwise your design will look flat instead of having a three-dimensional appearance. Extra golden rod, spray carnations, Singapore orchids, roses, freesias, golden ivy and privet have been used for this purpose. Also make sure at this stage that the foral foam is completely hidden from view by the strategic placement of leaves. At this point add the 'focal point' or centre of interest, in this case the lilies, making sure they are recessed properly.

Recessing means tucking plant material or flowers behind others to give depth. This takes away the more solid look which is evident when everything is on the same plane.

All that remains is to add a few extra buds and small flowers as the finishing touches. Make sure there is space around all your flowers. 'Leave room for the butterflies', as they say, and do remember the flower arranger's dictum—*if in doubt leave it out.*

Although this shape is arranged here in a tall container, it is equally as effective in a flat one.

ASYMMETRICAL TRIANGLE *See page 29*

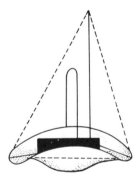

Container
Wicker basket

Mechanics
An oblong container which stands inside the basket has been fitted with four 4-pronged plastic holders for securing a largish piece of soaked floral foam. Top up with water.

Plant material
Larkspur, pinks, *Astilbe*, gladiolus, roses 'Silver Jubilee' and 'Dorothy Perkins', *Alchemilla mollis*, *Hosta fortunei* 'Albopicta' and *Polystichum setiferum*

Method
Tall pointed material such as larkspur makes an excellent outline for this shape of arrangement. Insert your main placement (which should be roughly one and a half times the length of your basket) left of centre to your design. The placements on either side which define its asymmetrical shape are cut to different lengths, the one on the left being much shorter than the one on the right (if you want a right-sided design the opposite will apply). These placements are angled

slightly forward to give depth. Insert additional transitional material, such as pinks, *Astilbe*, more larkspur and ferns to strengthen these lines keeping within the confines of the triangular shape. With this shape good balance can only be obtained if you use bolder plant material on the left of an imaginary vertical line from the apex to the base and slimmer material on the right. Try to put your placements in at different angles and planes to give a three-dimensional appearance. Now is a good time to add large hosta leaves at the base and place them flowing forward over the rim of the basket. Now insert your centre of interest, in this case I have used the gladiolus and the 'Silver Jubilee' roses. A few additional items can be added to finish off your design, such as *Alchemilla mollis* and tips of larkspur, taking care that some are recessed properly. Although this colour scheme is predominantly pink, the addition of touches of blue and acid green give extra interest.

In general you will find that asymmetrical arrangements give more opportunity for creativity than those which follow the strictly symmetrical pattern.

Although this design has been arranged in a 'flat' container any other type could have been used equally well.

HOGARTH CURVE *See page 33*

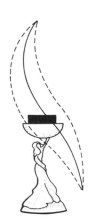

Container
Made from a spelter figurine with a candlecup holder affixed to its raised arm

Mechanics
A 6-pronged metal holder secures the soaked round of floral foam which stands well above the rim of the container. Top up with water.

Plant material
Astilbe, Alstroemeria, spray chrysanthemums, valerian, *Berberis thunbergii* 'Atropurpurea', *Prunus cerasifera* 'Atropurpurea' and *Eucalyptus gunnii*

Method
For this lazy S-shaped design it is essential to have the right outline material and the right container which must be tall

enough for the downward sweep of the arrangement. Two curved branches should be selected and here use has been made of *Berberis thunbergii* 'Atropurpurea' of just the right shape. Alternatively, pliable material such as broom and pussy-willow will lend themselves to manipulation into curves. Insert two pieces of curved material so that they form a continuous lazy S-shape or serpentine curve with the lower piece brought slightly forward so as not to present a flat basis for your design. Fill in the outline with some transitional material like *Astilbe*, spray chrysanthemums and *Alstroemeria* keeping them within its overall shape. Add some sprays of prunus and eucalyptus at the centre taking care to hide the floral foam and rim of the container. Now add the centre of interest which should not be too eye-catching and so prevent the eye moving up and down to explore the whole arrangement. Finish off the design by adding a few small flowers and buds. When placing flowers in any design try not to have them all facing the front. Turn a few so that they are in profile and thereby add another dimension to your design.

Beginners often have a problem with this shape of arrangement. Try to avoid ending up with a 'Catherine-wheel' effect by having the centre of the arrangement too round and compacted and merely suggesting the Hogarth curve with an upper piece of material bent to the right and the lower piece bent to the left. This is a common fault. Remember the widening to the centre and the tapering to the outsides should be gradual.

The Hogarth curve is named after the great English painter and engraver William Hogarth (1697–1764) who declared in his *Analysis of Beauty*, written in 1753, that this curve is 'the line of beauty'.

VERTICAL

Container
Tall 3-sided black pottery

Mechanics
The container is filled to about 2in, 5cm below rim with either soaked floral foam or sand with pinholder pushed firmly into this for safe anchorage. Top up with water.

Above: Hogarth curve

Above: Vertical

Plant material

Gladioli, roses 'Silver Jubilee' and *Hosta fortunei* 'Albopicta'

Method

For a vertical arrangement you will need a tall container to accentuate the upward thrust of this type of design. Vertical arrangements done in flat containers are never as impressive. For the outline it is best to choose sword-like leaves, for example iris, yucca or *Sansevieria* or flowers like gladioli or delphiniums to emphasize the upward movement, although all the placements need not necessarily be strictly vertical. If you choose to use single flowers, graduate them so that the smallest is at the top and the largest lower down. Insert your first placement, in this case the gladioli leaves, remembering

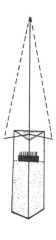

that the most pleasing height for this is usually one and a half times the height of the container. The two gladioli have been inserted close together so that they blend as one forming the slim top to the arrangement. The hosta leaves were added with three pointing upwards and two at the lower left coming forward. Care must be taken to keep any added leaves at the base close to the container as splayed-out leaves would spoil the shape of your design. Finally, add the focal point, in this case the two 'Silver Jubilee' roses, but any other eye-catching flowers would do instead. Dahlias, hydrangeas, chrysanthemums or lilies would all be suitable. Although this arrangement uses bold plant material it can be made with finer types of material, provided the design is kept tall and slim and has a dominant upward movement.

CRESCENT *See page 36*

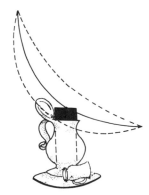

Container
Pewter tankard

Mechanics
An oblong piece of soaked floral foam has been pushed down to the base of the container with 2in, 5cm left to protrude above the rim. Top up with water.

Plant material
Gladioli *Astilbe*, pinks, hydrangeas and a spray of their leaves on a separate stem.

Method
As the pewter tankard on its own would have looked out of scale with the size of the arrangement it is placed on a pewter plate along with another tankard on its side to give added visual weight.

This is another shape which requires curved plant material for the outline. If you wish to use gladioli which are as straight as a poker, put them slantwise in a bucket overnight and by the morning the tips will have turned upwards and you will have your curved plant material (as seen in the illustration on page 36). Insert one of the curved gladioli stems to the left and one to the right to give a pleasing crescent outline. Remember that the right-hand placement should flow forwards to give depth to your design. Strengthen the outline by adding *Astilbe*, pinks and extra gladioli. The pink-tinted hydrangea leaves, which are on a separate stem, are placed at the centre just above the rim of the container making sure they hide the floral foam. Now insert the hydrangea along with the pinks to make the centre of interest. Finally, another smaller hydrangea is tucked in between the pinks to add a little more volume.

Always remember when floral foam is inserted deep into a container plenty of room must be left for topping-up with water. In this round container an oblong piece has been used so that there is ample room around it for water.

Should you wish, this shape of arrangement can be made in a flat container.

INVERTED CRESCENT *See page 37*

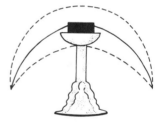

Container
White pottery stemmed container

Mechanics
A 6-pronged metal holder secures the soaked round of floral foam which stands above the rim of the container. Top up with water.

Plant material
Singapore orchids, spray carnations, *Campanula persicifolia*, *Philadelphus*, lilies, *Hosta undulata*, *Polystichum setiferum*, *Hedera helix* 'Harald'

Method
For this shape of design a tall stemmed container is essential to accommodate the downward sweep of its outline. Cut two gently curving stems about three-quarters of the height of the container and insert one at each side flowing downwards and slightly forward to establish the outline. Ferns are ideal for this as they have a natural curve, as do the Singapore orchids which, happily, are now freely available in most florists' shops. Next add a few pieces of ivy at the centre with a couple of hosta leaves which should be angled so that they flow over

Above: Inverted crescent

Left: Crescent

the rim of the container. These will not only hide the floral foam but give extra visual weight to this part of the design.

At this stage it is important to establish the height at the centre of the arrangement with short stems of flowers like carnations, campanulas and mock orange with a few pieces of foliage—ivy and hosta. Do not make the mistake of going too high with these placements otherwise your design will become a triangle rather than an inverted crescent.

Gradually build up the design with the smaller flowers and

buds on the outside and the larger flower towards the centre. Remember to have some backward placements to give a three-dimensional effect. Finally add the lilies as your centre of interest to complete the arrangement. This inverted crescent type of design lends itself well to the addition of one or two matching candles at the centre for a more festive look.

HORIZONTAL   *See page 40*

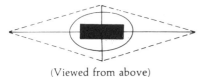

(Viewed from above)

Container
Silver dish

Mechanics
The dish has been reversed and on it has been placed a plastic dish fitted with a 6-pronged metal holder securing the soaked floral foam. Top up with water.

Plant material
Astilbe, Alstroemeria, two varieties of spray chrysanthemums, sweet peas, *Eucalyptus gunnii, Artemesia, Prunus cerasifera* 'Atropurpurea'

Method
Arrangements with a horizontal emphasis are particularly suitable for table centres and for displaying flowers on the mantleshelf. Their length, therefore, will be largely dictated by the amount of room you have for their display. The one designed for the mantleshelf will only be viewed from the front and will be greatly enhanced if the plant material flows forward over the shelf. The size and shape of the table and the amount of space available is your best guide for the centrepiece. In general a long slim line is best.

First cut your pointed material, in this case the artemesia, to the length required to establish the length of your arrangement. When these have been inserted strengthen this line with more *Artemesia* and a couple of stems of *Astilbe*. Now move to the centre of your design and establish the width with more of the same materials along with a few pieces of prunus and eucalyptus which are strategically placed to hide the floral foam. Remember to keep your arrangement low as you will want to be able to see the people sitting opposite as well as hear them! Add more *Alstroemeria*, sweet peas, and spray chrysanthemums at different angles with some recessed and all coming within the established outline. Finally strengthen the centre of your design with a grouping of chrysanthemums and *Alstroemerias*. With a table arrangement especially it is important to choose your flowers with care. Perfumed flowers are an advantage but beware of those not so sweet-smelling. The condition of your plant material is important, too, as it is open to close inspection. It is a good idea to sit down at the table when you have completed your centrepiece to make sure that none of your mechanics are showing.

For a special dinner party the addition of one or two lighted candles can add an extra sparkle to the occasion.

O V A L   *See page 41*

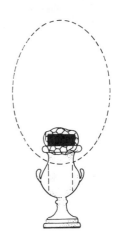

Container
Viridian coloured pottery urn

Mechanics
An oblong piece of soaked floral foam has been pushed down to the base of the container leaving at least 2in, 5cm above the rim. For extra security a piece of chicken wire covers the foam and has been fastened with wire. Top up with water.

Plant material
Lilies, foxgloves, *Astilbe*, *Astrantia*, hydrangeas, pinks, honeysuckle, roses 'Dorothy Perkins', larkspur, *Polystichum setiferum*, *Rosa rubrifolia*

Method
Many arrangements which we refer to as traditional, fall within an oval-shaped outline, especially those inspired by seventeenth-century Dutch and Flemish flower paintings. For this lavish style an urn makes an ideal container. Nowadays there are some attractive, lightweight specimens of fibreglass as well as the heavier pottery, metal and stone types. Garden flowers lend themselves beautifully to this style of arrangement which should be arranged naturally and gracefully. Its symmetrical balance should be achieved with a light touch and not contrived in any way.

For this design the outline is best made with flowers and

Above: Horizontal

Right: Oval

little extra foliage is used apart from that already on the flower stems. The tallest placement will again be about one and a half times the height of the container and here the lily stands proud at the top of the arrangement. When inserting your flowers the oval shape should be borne in mind but not over-emphasized as you do not want it to look as though it has been trimmed with shears! It does not really matter whether you start at the top of the arrangement and work down or make the outline first and fill in. Select your flowers and decide where you are going to place them with care so that not only is the colour combination pleasing but the different forms and textures add to the overall picture. This type of arrangement can be made in a grand scale for exhibition work. Then you could use a much larger and wider urn with flowers placed in tubes for extra height. A stone or marble base would be appropriate and this could be embellished with extra flowers, fruit, shells and even a bird's nest as was often used in the Dutch paintings.

This is the last of the *geometric shapes,* as they are termed. They should not be slavishly followed making ill-at-ease,

rather contrived arrangements, but used as a guide in making more free-and-easy designs.

The more you study flower arrangements of all styles and from all periods the more you will realize they can all be categorized within the basic art forms of the sphere, the cube, the ellipsoid and the pyramid.

PART TWO Other Styles

LANDSCAPE *See page 44*

Container
Two flat kidney-shaped pottery containers

Mechanics
One large and two small pinholders have been fastened to the base of the containers with floral fixative. Pieces of blue glass cover the pinholders. Top up with water.

Plant material
Dutch iris, flowering wild rush, leaves of *Iris pseudacorus* 'Variegata', *Hosta fortunei* 'Albopicta'

The landscape arrangement, a style which has developed in recent years, seems to be everyone's favourite, possibly because it is naturalistic and not contrived in any way. It can interpret the garden or the countryside, the lakeside or the seaside, the desert or some tropical paradise. The secret is to capture the atmosphere of your chosen theme with plant material from its environment and to exercise restraint; to suggest rather than spell out should be your aim.

Accessories are often incorporated in this type of arrangement and used with discretion they can add an extra dimension to the scene. But be warned, unless your chosen accessory is to scale, resist the temptation and leave it out. Many imaginative landscape designs have been spoilt for this reason alone.

A suitable base often helps to set the scene and untreated slivers or cross-cuts of wood are excellent for countryside and garden themes. Slate or stone may be more suitable for depicting the fells or mountainside, while large flat containers are best for waterside interpretations.

When using a base in a landscape design, the container should be of a size which can be hidden from view by the plant material or other suitable accessories like stones or shells. Visible containers are not often employed unless they add something to the scene. If you want to introduce moss, stones or shells don't overdo their use, this is another pitfall for the unwary.

The actual shape of your design will be dictated partly by the choice of materials and by the spirit you want to convey. The shape of the asymmetrical triangle seems to have an affinity with these landscape scenes but sometimes for waterside interpretations one or more vertical placements are more appropriate.

By way of illustration this waterside scene has been suggested by the two flat kidney-shaped containers lined with blue glaze. The smaller one is balanced on the corner of the larger to give water on two levels and the three placements of plant material complete the picture. A vertical group of flowering rush, Dutch iris, the beautifully marked yellow and green iris leaves together with similarly coloured hosta leaves gives height to the design while the two smaller placements at the lower level gives depth. The pinholders are well hidden with a few pieces of chunky blue glass, usually available from aquarium suppliers.

This style of arrangement is especially suitable for Christmas time. Children will be enchanted by a wintry scene of holly and evergreens sprayed with artificial snow with, perhaps, a robin or lantern to complete the scene.

POT-ET-FLEUR See page 45

Container
Viridian coloured large pottery container

Mechanics
Tubular containers for holding water for flowers.

Plant material
Dieffenbachia, Dracaena, Maranta, Adiantum (maidenhair fern) and two stems of lilies

The popularity of house plants for decorating the home has

increased enormously over the last few years. Florists, garden centres, supermarkets and chain stores all have extravagant collections but, to avoid disappointment, care must be taken in choosing the right plant for the right environment. Isolated plants dotted about do not have the same attraction as a grouping and even this way of display can be enlivened by the addition of choice fresh flowers. The *pot-et-fleur* style as it is called only came into being within the last twenty-five years and it is often featured in classes at flower shows. This is a very practical idea for the home as it can be a permanent feature and flowers can easily be added for special occasions.

There are two ways to group your plants: by removing the plants from their individual pots and replanting in a large container or by allowing the plants to remain in their individual pots and grouping them together in a large container with moss or peat to keep them in position.

If you decide on the first method it is important that all your chosen plants like the same conditions. It is no good including a plant which has to be kept on the dry side with one that prefers a moist situation. Apart from these considerations, it is also important to choose plants of varying heights, forms and textures which make an attractive colour grouping when put together.

Grouping plants together (out of their pots)
- Choose a container large enough to accommodate about four or five compatible plants. It should have sufficient depth to allow room for the roots to grow and enough width so that the leaves are not squashed. There are many types of suitable containers from pottery, fibreglass and plastic urns to large Victorian wash bowls and soup tureens as well as the more expensive antique copper bowls and deep pans.
- Place a $1\frac{1}{2}$in, 4cm thick layer of pebbles or crocks at the bottom of the container in order to provide some drainage and to prevent the roots becoming waterlogged (this is in place of a drainage hole).
- Crumble charcoal over the crocks to keep everything sweet and then partly fill with compost.
- Remove the plants carefully from the pots by turning them upside down and tapping on a hard surface.
- Decide on your arrangement of plants (some can be positioned on their sides) and when satisfied plant them carefully, filling in the gaps with compost. Make sure there

is a 1in, 2.5cm margin left to allow for watering.

● Insert your containers for the flowers where desired.

Grouping plants together (in pots)
The procedure is similar to the above. Arrange the potted plants in a pleasing group (not necessarily all upright) and pack in position with peat or moss. Add your containers for flowers as desired.

The illustration shows that it is not necessary to have a tall plant to give height to the arrangement, this can be done with flowers and these lilies were chosen to enhance the green and maroon colour combination.

C O N E   *See page 48*

Container
Pottery urn

Mechanics
Heavy pinholder, piece of cane or dowelling, two blocks of soaked floral foam, thin polythene (dry cleaner type) for covering foam to keep moist. Top up with water.

Plant material
Short stems of evergreens—box, ivy (some variegated), *Cupressus*, several stems of spray carnations, *Alchemilla mollis*, green grapes and *Hypericum* seedheads

Method
This is one of the easiest and most effective decorations for special occasions. It can either be arranged in a column or splayed out at the base, whichever best suits the situation. At Christmas time it is an ideal way of making a miniature tree using snippets of evergreens and decorating with baubles, artificial fruits or even small red bows. But if you want a more permanent decoration small-leaved glycerined or dried material can be used. Everlasting flowers like *Helichrysum*, dried hydrangea or *Achillea* together with small wired cones and clusters of seedheads could then be added. Special brown floral foam designed for dried and preserved materials should be used. Cone arrangements look best in some sort of footed container like an urn which should be very stable as it will have a considerable weight to bear when the design is

Above: Miniature

Left: Cone

complete. If your container is lightweight insert a few heavy stones between the floral foam and the container as ballast. Begin by putting a heavy pinholder on the base of your container and press down the first block of floral foam on to it. Now insert a piece of cane or dowelling (cut to size) into the pinholder through the centre of the vertical block. Then thread a second block of foam on top and trim to the required shape. To make sure that the foam does not dry out too quickly cover it with a thin piece of polythene. If, however, your arrangement is only for a single occasion this will not be necessary. Now insert short pieces of evergreens turning it round as you do so, until the cone is almost completely covered. Suitable materials include box, *Cupressus* and various ivies. Make sure to insert some of the larger leaves at the base to give it visual stability. If you have used the polythene covering you will probably need to use a metal skewer to puncture it before inserting your stems. Now add your flowers. Some arrangers like them in regimented patterns while others prefer them more casually placed; it is a matter of personal choice. Next add your clusters of grapes along with the *Hypericum* seedheads. If you have no old hair pins bend a few wires in a similar shape and use these for anchoring the grapes. Finally, a froth of *Alchemilla mollis* is added to lighten the overall effect.

This style is reminiscent of the Byzantine period when stylized cones of foliage, flowers and fruits as well as garlands and wreaths were much used for decoration.

MINIATURE *See page 49*

Container
Small sliver of wood

Mechanics
Soaked floral foam in bottle top

Plant material
Golden rod, *Lysimachia clethroides*, tomato flowers, *Lonicera nitida*, *Chamaecyparis*, box, fern, *Cotoneaster horizontalis* berries

PETITE *See page 52*

Container
Small wooden base

Mechanics
Tiny pinholder in small aerosol top

Plant material
Chamaecyparis, *Euphorbia*, *Acaena*, heather, montbretia seedheads, *Alchemilla mollis*

Miniature arrangements are always popular with the public at shows but unless you have a special spot where they can be seen to full advantage they are rarely done for home decoration.

They should be a miniaturized version of a full-scale arrangement as though viewed down the wrong end of a telescope. They must be perfect in every detail with the scale of each and every part correct. If a flower or leaf is too large in relation to the other material or for the container, or if it is the other way round then the illusion will be lost. It is very much like viewing items in a doll's house. If they are not all exactly to scale then the illusion of viewing a full-sized room is lost.

Mechanics
The problem with creating small arrangements is to find suitable ways of anchoring the tiny pieces of plant material. If containers with narrow necks are used then no mechanics are necessary. However, if the necks are wider a small piece of floral foam can be inserted. Sand can also be used. For low containers you might be lucky enough to find tiny pinholders. Failing this a small piece of sheet lead shaped like a tiny crown can be used to hold the foam in place but it must be hidden with plant material or tiny pebbles. A pair of tweezers are best for inserting the plant material since fingers can easily squash the stems. Small scissors, too, are best for cutting your materials and an eye-dropper is ideal for filling up the container with water.

Containers
In addition to the miniature vases which you can sometimes buy, items like small perfume bottles, thimbles, lipstick cases, pill-boxes and bottle tops can all be utilized.

Bases
Small wooden cocktail mats, cross-cuts of wood, small flat pebbles and pieces of slate, cosmetic jar lids, or thick card cut to shape and covered with fabric can all be used as bases. It is a case of using one's ingenuity.

Plant material
The selection of the right plant material is an art in itself. It is usually easier to find tiny leaves and bits of foliage than suitable flowers. However, a scavenge around the garden will often produce unsuspected treasures. Rock plants are especially useful as well as individual florets from multiple

blooms like *Alyssum, Arabis, Achillea,* candytuft, *Nepeta,* veronica, *Heuchera,* golden rod and some of the flowering shrubs. Tiny seedheads are useful and tendrils from some climbers make perfect modern outlines.

Accessories

These are usually permitted with these types of arrangement and tiny carved and ceramic figures are suitable, provided their scale is correct. The usually accepted sizes for these arrangements are:

Miniature—An exhibit not exceeding 4in, 10cm in width, depth and height. This measurement does not apply to diagonal dimension.

Petite—An exhibit not exceeding 9in, 23cm in width, depth and height. This measurement does not apply to the diagonal dimension.

When entering these classes in shows try to keep your arrangements simple and remember all the principles are exactly the same as those when making a full-sized design. It is certainly a test of patience and nimble fingers but it is fun to be able to do the small as well as the great.

Left: Petite

4

More Aspects of Flower Arrangement

DRIFTWOOD

The term *driftwood* used in the flower arrangement sense includes any type of dried wood, roots or bark and need not necessarily have been carried by water as the literal definition would suggest. For the purpose of competitive work it is classified as dried plant material.

Driftwood has always had a special fascination for flower arrangers with its endless variety of shapes, textures and colours—no two pieces are alike—and best of all, it costs nothing. Whether you are interested in traditional, naturalistic or the modern style of arranging, you will find it complements them all. It is so economical to use as it will enable you to make quite a sizeable design with just a few well chosen flowers and foliage.

Where to find driftwood
The best places for seeking driftwood are along the high-water mark on the shore, on river banks (especially after flood water), on lake shores and in the countryside. Each particular environment has its own special type of treasure. The beach usually provides well-rounded and bleached pieces which have been tossed about in the sea, maybe for many years. Wood found by the river and lakeside as a result of winter storms is of the more angular variety, usually broken branches and tree roots. Driftwood from the countryside has a more chunky appearance and consists mainly of partially

rotted tree stumps and larger branches. This type of wood is usually harder to find as it is often three-quarters hidden in the undergrowth. Always examine carefully any wood which you are contemplating bringing home. If it contains too much rotted or any worm-eaten substance leave it behind, no matter how exciting it may look at first sight.

Preparation of driftwood
Remove all the loose bits of wood, moss and debris with a wire brush. An old screwdriver or long pointed knife can be used to scrape out some of the deeper crevices. When this has been done hose it down under a high pressure jet and let it dry naturally. It is always safer to treat all driftwood with a woodworm fluid to make sure no pests are brought into the house.

Don't be in too much of a hurry to trim and alter the shape of the wood, consider all the possibilities before you start. You might decide first to trim off uninteresting bits and pieces. Later you may decide to take off a section from one side and add it to the other to make a more pleasing shape. Alternatively, you may decide to take two or three similar pieces of wood and peg and glue them together to make an eye-catching free-standing 'sculpture'.

Driftwood left in its natural state as fashioned by the elements takes some beating but you can polish, stain, varnish, bleach and spray-paint as you wish.

Mechanics for driftwood
Securing driftwood in your arrangements is an art in itself and calls for great ingenuity if you wish to display your pieces to their best advantage. The easiest pieces to use, of course, are those which are by chance free-standing. Very rarely do we find such pieces but sometimes by adding or cutting away a small section of the wood it can be made to stand without support. This means that there are no mechanics to be hidden and you are free to add your flowers and foliage as you wish.

Sometimes a large chunk of wood only needs levelling to make it stand firmly, but where to cut the wood is the question. The best way is to dip the piece of wood at the correct angle into a bowl of water and wait until a watermark is left, lift out and mark with chalk. When the wood is dry simply saw along the line. An uneven piece can often be stabilized by adding a wedge of wood. Light pieces are much easier to deal with. If the wood is reasonably soft it can be impaled on to a pinholder but if it is too hard for this

See page 56
Two handsome pieces of similarly coloured and textured driftwood combine to make an antler-like outline for this eye-catching design. The two *Kniphofia* spikes follow the line of the driftwood and the grouping of dahlias, golden rod, variegated yew and spotted laurel stabilizes the forceful upward thrust of the wood.

See page 57
Two dramatically shaped, weather-bleached pieces of manzanita wood combine to make a natural piece of modern sculpture, highlighted by the round pink heads of hydrangea and the bold grey Onopordum *leaves.*

treatment, try slotting it into a piece of hollow stem. Dried teasel or hogweed are ideal for this purpose but remember to cut the stem with a junior hacksaw. If you use secateurs it will split. If a piece of wood is too thick for this method give it the 'peg-leg' treatment. Turn it upside down and drill a hole from the base down the centre of the wood for at least 1in, 2cm. Gently knock in and glue a piece of dowelling of the same diameter cut to the length desired. A short piece will be sufficient for insertion into a pinholder or floral foam. A longer length will be required for use in a tall container. Specially made driftwood clamps can be purchased and they provide another way of holding reasonably sized pieces of wood.

There are three types available:

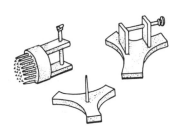

- A lead disc embedded with a screw thread which is simply screwed into the wood.
- An inverted pinholder clamp into which the wood is screwed tightly so that it can be impaled on to a normal pinholder.
- A screw clamp on a heavy lead base suitable only for well-balanced pieces of wood.

If there is no other alternative then a heavy piece of wood can be set permanently in either plaster of Paris or cement. The disadvantage with this way of fixing is (a) it can only be used in one way and (b) a large placement of flowers and foliage will be required to hide the mechanics. When creating modern designs, especially imaginative ways of anchoring wood are of paramount importance and these are discussed in the final chapter of the book.

FRUIT AND VEGETABLES

The sight of a well-designed window display in a greengrocer's shop draws the eye as much as any florist's window especially when the soft fruit season is at its peak the window becomes a kaleidoscope of colour. Succulent strawberries, bright shining cherries, curvaceous peaches and nectarines, green furry gooseberries and kiwi fruit, rich purple plums or damsons and jewel-like strings of redcurrants— who can resist them? So why not include some in your arrangements and have the pleasure of looking at them before they are finally eaten?

We automatically think of harvest time for arranging fruits and vegetables but this should not preclude them from appearing in our decorative scheme of things for the home at other times of the year. Fruit in particular lends itself to being arranged with flowers and foliage in quite sophisticated designs, whereas vegetables are more in keeping with kitchen, barbecue or country cottage-type arrangements.

Selection

When choosing fruit or vegetables for display two things are essential—they should be absolutely fresh and unblemished. In fact under-ripe fruit is best as it will not only last longer but quite often the colour in the ripening process is far more interesting. Lemons, oranges and bananas with a touch of green are much more attractive, as are ripening capsicums with their many colours. The size, shape and texture of fruit and vegetables are equally important factors when considering how to use them. Large items such as pineapples, melons, cabbages and squashes should be used sparingly whilst the smaller round items like apples, oranges and peaches can be used more liberally. This also applies to vegetables. Do not overdo the number of varieties you choose—after all, you want it to look like an arrangement and not a market stall!

Preparation

The preparation of your chosen fruit or vegetables is an important factor in their display. Wash and polish most fruit with a soft duster with the exception of those which have a natural bloom such as grapes, peaches and plums. To improve the blush on apples or pears you can gently rub on a little lipstick to make them look more tempting. Make sure the vegetables are scrupulously clean and presentable, taking off some of the outside leaves from green vegetables, peeling the top skin off onions and shallots, and scrubbing root crops.

Containers

The choice of container will largely be governed by the type of materials which you have selected as well as by their final situation for display. When displaying vegetables wooden or marble bases, baskets, trays or large flat bowls would be appropriate and although these would also be suitable for fruit something a little more sophisticated could be chosen to go with their more delicate nature. Silver dishes, glass compotes or even an elegant epergne can be considered. If you have your heart set on an unsuitably deep container, don't despair.

Above
Apricots, peaches, nectarines and grapes suggested the colour scheme for this arrangement. The outline material includes *Lonicera nitida* 'Baggesen's Gold', *Berberis thunbergii* 'Atropurpurea', *Rosa rubrifolia*, golden privet, and *Hedera helix* 'Buttercup Lemon spray carnations, 'The Flower Arranger' rose and berries from Hypericum add the final touch.

It can still be used as long as you can raise the fruit in some way. This can be achieved by using crumpled paper or chicken wire or a dry block of floral foam. Sometimes a securely fastened upturned bowl can do the trick.

Make sure the fruits and vegetables do not come in contact with water or they will soon rot. Always include a separate container to hold your flowers and foliage. If only a few flowers and a couple of leaves are to be used, they are best inserted in orchid tubes which can be secreted amongst the fruit. This is an ideal way to do a quick dinner table arrangement which usually creates more interest than more conventional centrepieces. With this in mind, why not surprise your guests with a design of flowers and frosted fruits? They are easy to prepare. Simply paint over your chosen fruits with beaten egg-white, liberally dredge them with caster sugar and leave to dry in a warm place. A silver dish piled high with green and black frosted grapes with a few clematis flowers and trails of ivy secreted in orchid tubes among the fruits can look

delightful. Another happy combination is of peaches, nectarines and apricots with some small roses and ivy trails added for highlights.

Mechanics

In fruit and vegetable designs mechanics are all-important. If the fruits and vegetables are not securely anchored, a domino-effect disaster can strike. Wooden skewers and cocktail sticks are better than wires for this job as they will not spoil the fruit for eating later. However, strong stub wire can be used for holding grapes in position by threading it through the bunch and twisting the end on to a skewer for easy placement. Cherries can be effectively displayed by twisting thin stub wires around the individual stems, grouping them together in your hand and finally binding the cluster with floral tape. Pineapples can be held high at the top of an arrangement on a tripod of three wooden kebab skewers which are usefully long for this purpose. Most other fruits can

Above
Herbs and vegetables are the main items of this arrangement. The vegetables placed on a wooden base consist of cabbage, peas, carrots, onions and celery. The herbs include apple mint, parsley, fennel and rue along with *Allium* seedheads. The non-edible subjects are *Acanthus*, variegated yew, *Euonymus fortunei* 'Silver Queen', *Hosta fortunei* 'Aureomarginata' and *Fatsia japonica*.

61

be secured to each other with cocktail sticks, but vegetables usually require something a little stronger like skewers. Insert half of the cocktail stick or skewer into the fruit or vegetables and push the other half into its neighbour. Another way to display these items is to make them into a cone. This makes a delightful display for a buffet table and the method of making one is described on page 47.

Fruit and vegetables are not difficult to arrange but their solid, heavy forms require skilful handling. Study the shapes and sizes carefully before you start and be selective. Round shapes make a good centre of interest and this enables you to build outwards with graduating shapes and sizes for a pleasing effect. Play around with the various items in different positions and when you are finally satisfied that your placements are the best that can be obtained secure them. The same principles apply as in all flower arranging where form, interesting textures and beautiful colouring each play their part.

ACCESSORIES

How to integrate into designs
There are so many different facets to flower arranging and the use of accessories to enhance your arrangements in the home is one well worth exploring. We all have our own particular treasures; some of them may be precious antiques and others merely souvenirs with happy associations. With a little ingenuity and know-how many of them can be incorporated into designs to provide an eye-catching set piece.

The term 'accessory' for show purposes is anything which is added to plant material to form an exhibit. Plant material in its natural state is never an accessory but plant material which has been *altered* from its original state into another form like, for example, a corn dolly or a carved wooden figure is termed an accessory. Happily, the finer points which we have to comply with in show work need not restrict us when we are arranging purely for our own enjoyment in the home.

When thinking of accessories, figurines immediately spring to mind but they can be virtually anything which would not look incongruous—antique lamps, precious pieces of china, coloured glass and crystal, fancy carved candles—the list is endless. It is fun to experiment with various items in the home which you might never have contemplated using in this way. However, before you decide on an accessory for a particular situation, make sure it is in keeping with the style of the room in which it is to be displayed. You would not choose a rustic garden trug with trowel design for a sophisticated style of room nor would you think of displaying Crown Derby in a sun loggia. Your choice should be aesthetically pleasing in every way.

Scale

This is the most important factor to consider in this style of arranging. Unless you intend to make miniature arrangements do not consider any small trinkets as they will look ridiculous with averaged-sized flowers. Once you have chosen your accessory you then have to decide how to incorporate it into your design. If it is small you may wish to raise it up in some way to make it appear more dominant; if it is larger you might want to hide part of it. Whatever you decide, put your accessory in place before arranging your flowers. A base of some kind is useful to unify your grouping and this should be selected with care so that it is in complete accord with the chosen 'theme'. For example, you would not think of using a velvet covered base with driftwood, nor would you choose to display silver on an acrylic base. If you are using more than one accessory, make sure that the size relationship between them is acceptable. The scale of flowers to accessory is of paramount importance. Bold accessories can be enhanced with equally bold plant material but dainty figurines must have petite flowers and delicate foliage. Bear in mind always that the scale of every item used in the completed composition should be in tune with each other.

Style

This relates to the compatibility of your chosen accessory and the type of your arrangement. A modern piece of sculpture would demand a modern concept in the overall design while some sort of period piece would be more in keeping with the traditional style of arrangement. The type of flowers, too, would need to be matched with the style of the arrangement. For example, a Victorian piece would make a more telling picture if the flowers and foliage used were popular in that period while something with a Far Eastern flavour would be better suited to the more stylized oriental way of arranging flowers.

See page 64
The colours of the cockerel are picked up in this arrangement using common-or-garden flowers which are in keeping with the rustic theme. Orange *Alstroemerias* and the quill-petalled *Inula* supply the orange and yellow while the *Hosta fortunei* 'Aureomarginata', ivy and *Fatsia japonica* make up the green colouring.

See page 65
The flowing form of this figure suggests the outline for the design. A tall stem of *Francoa* ('Maiden's Wreath') gives height to this arrangement and it is caught up in the figure's hand as though he is carrying a banner. Smaller pieces of this delightful flower along with lilies, freesias, spray carnations and leaves of *Choisya ternata* complete the picture.

Colour

You may choose your accessory purely because it harmonizes with the colour scheme of a room. In this case you would select flowers and foliage of tints, tones and shades of the particular hue to further emphasize the overall scheme. On the other hand you might wish to have something which would give more colour impact and choose a contrasting or complementary colour scheme. Colours which lie opposite on the colour circle would give this effect. For example, a predominantly green colour scheme could be highlighted with vibrant reds, or a blue room with a striking orange design.

The use and appreciation of colour is another personal choice—one person's likes are another's dislikes—and so experiment with alternatives and never be restricted by preconceived ideas.

When you have completed your design it is a good idea to stand back and assess it dispassionately. Ask yourself is it suitable for the situation? Is the colour scheme well thought out? Has the overall composition been guided by your knowledge of the elements and principles of good design? Has the accessory been well integrated? Is all the plant material in pristine condition? If you can say 'yes' to all these questions you can be sure you have a perfect arrangement.

The use of accessories takes imagination as well as restraint. It is totally absorbing and the thrill one feels on achieving a satisfactory outcome is hard to describe.

PRESERVED AND DRIED MATERIALS

Every arranger should have a collection of dried and preserved plant material as it can be useful in so many ways. As well as using them on their own, these items can be effectively incorporated with fresh flowers at that time of the year when foliage from the garden is at a low ebb.

One of the most popular kinds of arrangement we see in the autumn and winter months are chrysanthemums arranged with glycerined beech—a wonderfully effective combination. Another popular idea for these everlasting treasures is to make pictures, plaques or swags for permanent decoration. This particular side of arranging, along with the making of pressed flower pictures, greeting cards, calendars, floral paperweights as well as seed collages is a hobby in itself. At Christmas time, too, dried plant material can be spray-painted or glittered for very effective arrangements. It seems that there is no end to its uses and new ways for display are constantly being discovered.

Preserving with glycerine

Plant material preserved this way lasts much longer as it remains supple where most other methods leave you with a brittle and more breakable product. Glycerine can easily be obtained from the chemist's in different sized bottles. When

Suitable plant material for glycerining	
FOLIAGE AND LEAVES	FLOWERS AND SEEDHEADS
*Aspidistra** *Ficus elastica**	*Clematis vitalba*
Aucuba (spotted *Grevillea robusta*	*Eryngium* (sea holly)
laurel) *Hedera* (ivy)†	*Garrya elliptica*
beech *Laurus nobilis*	hydrangea
Bergenia† (laurel)	lime flowers
broom *Magnolia*	*Moluccella laevis*
Buxus (box) *Mahonia*	sycamore fruits
Camellia *Pittosporum*	*Castanea* (sweet
Choisya ternata *Quercus* (oak)	chestnut) fruits
Cotoneaster *Rhododendron*	hornbeam seeds
Elaeagnus Solomon's seal	iris seed pods
*Fatsia japonica** *Sorbus aria*	*Papaver orientale*
ferns (whitebeam)	(poppy)
× *Fatshedera*	teasel

*These subjects are unable to absorb the glycerine mixture quickly enough and their tips dry out prematurely. To prevent this happening mop or spray them with the mixture before standing in the liquid and repeat the process regularly until they have taken. This is a rather messy operation but well worthwhile.

†These subjects with tougher leaves leaves respond better to total immersion in the glycerine mixture in a flat dish until they change colour. Carefully store your glycerined material in cardboard boxes in a dry situation. Heat may cause the leaves to shrivel while dampness can cause mildew so *do not* use polythene bags for storage.

See page 68
This traditional arrangement of dried and preserved materials is made up from items most arrangers have in their gardens. The dark brown foliage is of *Mahonia bealii, Eucalyptus* and *Azara* while the biscuit-coloured foliage is *Choisya ternata* and *Ruscus*. Both leek and skeletonized poppy seedheads give a change of form while the artichoke flowers and *Physalis* add the finishing touches.

See page 69
Bolder types of dried and preserved plant material lend themselves to a modern interpretation, and imported materials often fall into this category. The tall pointed leaves, cycas and fan palms, the unusual seed-pods and the made-up 'lilies' are all foreign but the pieces of monkey puzzle (*Araucaria*) and *Molucella laevis* are home-grown.

you have decided on the quantity you need, pour the glycerine into a tall heavy container, add double the volume of hot water and mix well. It is also a good idea to add a teaspoonful of mild disinfectant to prevent mildew forming. The mixture lasts indefinitely so keep topping it up as it is used. Before you place any material in the liquid cut off any damaged or surplus leaves and slit up the ends of woody stems for about 2in, 5cm to help absorbtion. Foliage that is mature is the best for this purpose otherwise it will flop before it has time to absorb the glycerine mixture. You will find some subjects take much longer to absorb the liquid but once the leaves have changed from green to brown remove them and hang upside down to make sure the mixture reaches the tips of the foliage. Leaves and foliage which have been preserved can be lightened in colour by standing them in sunshine. Beech particularly responds to this method and so it is possible to have it in various shades from a light orangey tint to darkest brown.

Air drying plant material
Many plants and flowers will dry naturally out of doors but if you want to use them in your arrangements they must be in perfect condition and this calls for a little extra time and

Suitable plants air drying			
FLOWERS		SEEDHEADS	GRASSES
artichoke	lavender	*Agapanthus*	*Briza maxima*
Acanthus	*Liatris*	*Allium*	*Cortaderia*
Amaranthus	*Polygonum*	*Angelica*	*Festuca*
caudatus	*Sedum*	*Clematis*	*Hordeum*
Anaphalis	*Solidago*	*Lunaria*	Job's tears
Artemesia	all the	*Montbretia*	millet
clary	immortelles	*Nigella*	cereals
Crocosmia	*Helichrysum*	*Nicandra*	wheat
cardoon	*Helipterum*	*Physalis*	barley
Delphinium	*Limonium*	*Rumex*	oats
Echinops	*Xeranthemum*		

Note: *Achilleas*, heathers, hydrangeas and *Proteas* are better dried gradually while standing in 1in, 2.5cm of water.

trouble. It is important to cut your materials at the right time for good results. Most flowers are best gathered on a dry day and they should be unblemished and not fully open. Seedheads are best cut when they are beginning to dry on the plant, while bulrushes, pampas grass and thistles are best cut when half developed. Tie them together in small bunches and hang upside down; an old clothes rack makes an excellent drying frame. Any dry and preferably warm place with a free circulation of air gives the best results.

Desiccants

In this drying method the water content of the plant material is withdrawn and absorbed by various substances such as alum, borax, sand or silica gel. Most arrangers agree that the silica gel method is the best. It is used for multi-petalled flowers such as roses, camellias and many others which cannot be dried in any other way. The results are fragile and they can only be used for specialized work and only patient people should attempt this technique. First pick your plant material (just prior to maturity) and cut off the stem within 1in, 2.5cm of the flower head. Put a 1–2in, 2.5–5cm layer of desiccant into a suitable tin. Into this insert the stem and gently cover the flower head by pouring more desiccant over and around it using a pointed stick or paint-brush to make sure every crevice is filled. Cover with a layer 1–2in, 2.5–5cm of desiccant before replacing the lid. Tape to make sure it is airtight. Put in a warm place such as an airing cupboard to dry. How many flowers you do at a time will depend on their size and the size of the container. Different types of flowers will take different lengths of time to dry out and in this instance experience is the great teacher.

Drying by pressing

Material preserved by this method is best for making pictures and greetings cards because of its inevitable flat appearance. Pick your materials on a dry day and arrange them carefully on blotting paper or newspaper. Press using a special flower press, under books or bricks, or even under the carpet. Check frequently and change the paper if it becomes damp. Plant material required for pictures needs to be pressed for at least three months. If you wish to press three-dimensional specimens they should be suitably dismantled, pressed and re-assembled for use.

SHOW WORK

Schedules for any show be it NAFAS (National Association of Flower Arrangement Societies), WI (Womens' Institute), TG (Townswomens' Guild) or horticultural, all include their own particular rules. It is most important that they are read carefully and digested before you even start thinking about your exhibits so you will not be disqualified for some minor infringement.

In general, the latest edition of the NAFAS Handbook of Schedule Definitions is considered to be the definitive arbiter of flower arranging practice and is often referred to in flower arranging practice and is often referred to in flower arranging schedules by other organisations.

A well thought-out schedule should include both decorative and interpretive classes and as a general rule they are given titles as a source of inspiration for the exhibitor. Sometimes the class title is given entirely on its own which allows exhibitors free rein to use the natural plant material they wish with or without accessories. At other times the schedule may give the class title and a style of exhibit (e.g. Landscape) or, alternatively, state whether specific types of plant material are to be used and whether accessories are permissible. The size of the space allocated to each exhibit will be given including the width, depth and height along with the staging details which will include the type and colour of any backing.

If, after reading the show schedule through, you have any queries whatsoever don't hesitate to get in touch with the Show Secretary who will be happy to clarify any particular points of which you are not sure.

Most flower arrangers start exhibiting by entering their club or local horticultural show. This is an excellent idea for in this way you will gain experience and confidence and when you have had some success at this level you can move on to higher things. The demands of entering the larger horticultural and area shows and, of course, the national competitions are much greater but you will be able to take it in your stride because of the experience you have gained on the way up.

Opposite
This seascape design is an example of the type which could be entered in a class calling for an exhibit evocative of a maritime theme. Remember the plant material should predominate and here the driftwood, sea-wrack, sea-weed, *Echeveria* and *Artemisia* have a greater impact than the accessories of sea-fan, star-fish, shells and mummified crab.

Even the most experienced arrangers will sometimes suffer from 'show nerves' but as soon as you start the actual arranging in the company of others you will find the whole experience totally stimulating and enjoyable.

How to enter

Obtain your schedule well in advance of the show date and study it well before you decide which classes to enter. If you are a beginner it is better to start by entering only one class with a simple straightforward arrangement so that you will not be over anxious and unable to enjoy the occasion. The more experienced arrangers, however, can easily cope with several exhibits. Make a point of sending your entry in early to avoid disappointment as some of the more popular classes are often over subscribed. On acceptance note down in your diary staging and dismantling times and dates along with a note to remind you to order flowers well beforehand from your florist.

Planning your exhibit

Most classes these days are given titles and call for interpretive work which is much more demanding than the old-style schedule which might have simply called for an arrangement of five flowers and foliage. Make sure that everything you wish to use in your exhibit is permissible. Some classes call for fresh flowers only, while others give you complete freedom with only the class title to interpret. Take time to consider the full meaning of your chosen title and do some research to make sure you know all about the subject. It is absolutely essential that the meaning should be obvious and anything which is obscurely symbolic and which needs to be explained to the viewer is to be avoided. It is a good idea to jot down ideas as they come to you, maybe about flowers which would be especially appropriate, possible accessories or even bases, anything at all to do with your exhibit. Always have one or two mock-ups well in advance so that your ideas can be put to the test and if found wanting there is still an opportunity to change or re-adjust them. The size of your niche together with the colour of your backing will be started on the schedule and it is worthwhile making a similar one to practice with at home. Unless you do this it will be difficult to get your staging just right at the show. Your exhibit should not be too small for the size of your niche nor should it be too large with foliage touching the sides.

Final preparations for the show
Attention to detail is all-important. Collect and prepare your plant material in good time and check that you have sufficient buckets or plastic lined boxes for their transportation. Make sure that your containers and mechanics are well prepared and will remain securely fixed for the duration of the show. Make a check list and tick off as you load the car to make sure you have everything you require for all your exhibits. As well as taking a few extra flowers and foliage add floral foam, a large pinholder, duster, mopping-up sponge, wires, watering can, a piece of plastic sheeting and don't forget the schedule!

Interpretive work
The best exhibits are those where the plant material and not the accessories tell the story. It is a sad fact that if you took away the accessories in many of the exhibits at shows today it would be difficult to say what the exhibit was supposed to be depicting. Whilst it will not always be possible to tell the whole story with plant material alone, one or more well chosen accessories are perfectly acceptable as long as they have something to contribute and are in scale with the rest of the items in the exhibit. Even if you have half a dozen appropriate accessories, be selective and choose with care; understatement is better than overstatement. When you do the mock-up of your exhibit try to use different levels and give a good "three-dimensional" effect. Remember, space is another important factor, both the space around the design and the space within. Avoid clutter at all costs. Your choice of plant material will be governed by its colour, form and texture which should further enhance the interpretation of your theme. If you are using any drapes they should be in perfect condition, painted backgrounds should not intrude and, last but not least, your plant material should always predominate over the accessories.

Judging
Adherence to the show schedule is of vital importance and if these are flouted in any way then disqualification is the only

outcome. Other aspects the judge will consider are whether the plant material predominates, whether the exhibit interprets the title, whether good use has been made of all the design principles in the staging of the exhibit, whether the plant material is in tip-top condition, whether the backgrounds or drapes are suitable and finally, whether your exhibit has that certain something which makes it stand out from all the rest.

FESTIVE OCCASIONS

Ideas for arrangements for special occasions
Flower arrangements for special festivals, family anniversaries and individual celebrations are great fun to do and add an extra dimension to the occasion. Christmas is the one time when flower arrangers especially like to indulge their fantasies and create extravagant arrangements but there are many other times when a little extra thought and trouble can make an occasion memorable.

Some flowers have special associations like red roses for Valentine's Day and white lilies for Easter. Accessories, too, can be brought out to give extra meaning and sparkle to your arrangements. But don't leave your preparations until the last moment; think about them well in advance and get any bases, accessories and containers ready in good time. If you want to do something very special make a mock-up beforehand to ensure your ideas are feasible and that the result is exactly what you are aiming for. If it is not, it will give you time to change your ideas and make another attempt to get it just right. Then when the special event arrives, all you have to do is order the flowers.

Here are a few thoughts and ideas for arranging flowers for festive occasions in the home.

Birthdays
Your style of arrangement should be geared to the age of the party-goer. Young children are intrigued with arrangements incorporating sweets and lollipops while brightly coloured modern designs or dangling mobiles would be more in keeping with a disco. Barbecues or any *al fresco* entertaining are always enlivened by the addition of groupings of pot plants and arrangements incorporating fruits or even vegetables. Dinner and luncheon party arrangements should

Opposite
This landscape arrangement suggests autumn in the countryside and could be entered in a class with a title such as 'Nature's Bounty' or 'The Squirrel's Larder'. The bold outline is made up from several pieces of driftwood placed on a large sliver of wood. The flowers, fruits and foliage are all evocative of the autumn theme.

be kept low so the guests on one side of the table will not be cut off from the guests on the other side by a barricade of flowers. However, buffet parties call for tall arrangements in stable containers with the flowers well above the level of the table and clear of the food. Tall matching pyramids of fruits and flowers would make eye-catching displays for such an occasion.

Your choice of flowers for all these types of designs should, of course, tie up with the colour scheme of the room and all the table linen, candles and other accessories should be carefully chosen to harmonize.

Bonfire night
Children as well as grown-ups are always fascinated by any kind of interpretative arrangement and Guy Fawkes night lends itself to this kind of thing. Choose plant material which simulates fire by using red and orange flowers; smoke can be suggested by pampas grass or old man's beard and fireworks by bulrushes which resemble rockets and *Allium, Angelica* or *Agapanthus* seedheads which look like exploding starburst fireworks. A 'guy' could easily be made and added to the design to delight the children.

Christenings
Some people prefer white arrangements for christenings whilst others like pink or blue depending on whether it is a boy or girl. An old wooden crib would make an excellent container or an arrangement could be made to incorporate some appropriate accessory, like a stork or a family heirloom such as an ivory and silver teething-ring. Small, delicate and unsophisticated flowers which have an air of innocence are an excellent choice.

Christmas
This is the one time of the year when everyone has a go! Some people are traditionalists and always decorate their homes with evergreens and fresh flowers. Green, red and white with maybe a touch of silver and gold are their chosen colours. Others prefer to have arrangements to match their room colour schemes and nowadays it is easy to buy artificial plant material in a kaleidoscope of colours. This is the only time of the year when most arrangers are prepared to use these synthetic materials. The amount of time available also plays a large part in the choice of decoration. For the traditionalist time must be found for constantly topping-up your

arrangements, renewing fading flowers and sweeping up fallen pine needles. If time is at a premium the alternative is arrangements of artificial plant material which can be made up well in advance and brought out for the festive season. Many people love to make garlands of evergreens for the mantleshelf and staircase and swags or wreaths for the front door. Time-consuming maybe, but well worthwhile for the atmosphere they create. A special decoration for the dinner table is a must and fruit piled high with added foliage and flowers always looks good—but remember it must not encroach too much as the food is the main attraction for many on Christmas Day.

Easter
If there are children in the house then Easter eggs, fluffy chickens and Easter bunnies can be featured in your arrangements but for older people the symbolism of Easter may be more appropriate with designs to suggest either the crucifixion or the resurrection of Christ.

Halloween
Black cats, witches, bats, bright shining apples and hollowed-out turnip or pumpkin lamps resembling grotesque faces are all associated with this festival. How cats, witches and bats should be represented is a matter of using your own imagination and ingenuity. If you can depict them by cleverly using only natural plant material, so much the better. But on such an occasion you can make them out of anything at all, even black paper cut-outs. The hollowing out of turnips and pumpkins needs no instruction—just a sharp knife and hard graft.

May Day
The first of May still has its rural associations in spite of the more solemn May Day parades in other countries. We think of children dancing round the colourful Maypole, baskets of country flowers, ribbons galore and the rustic festival it once was.

St Valentine's Day
14 February is always worth celebrating by the young at heart, with its associations with blood-red roses, cupids, arrow-pierced hearts, pretty lace-edged cards and dainty shepherd and shepherdess figurines, all of which would be suitable to incorporate in your designs for this special day.

See page 80
This 'Bon Voyage' design is for friends returning to the Far East. Two Balinese carved heads are surrounded by lush vegetation and although it is home-grown it is nevertheless evocative of this Pacific paradise.

See page 81
Christmas is the one time arrangers are prepared to accept artificial plant material in their arrangements. A splendid Madonna and Child is the centrepiece of this design and around it are grouped artificial plant materials in green, cream and gold. A curving piece of ivy frames the sculpture and at the same time holds a gilded cherub aloft.

Weddings
Most flowers arranged for weddings are required away from the home, both in the church and where the reception is being held. Nevertheless, some arrangements at home—especially in the bride's home— are still important to set the scene for the great day.

Wedding anniversaries
Each anniversary has its own special connotations from wood at five years to gold at fifty and it's fun to make appropriate arrangements to celebrate each occasion. Naturally we make a fuss of great landmarks—the Silver Wedding at twenty-five years, Ruby at forty years and Golden at fifty years. For such special occasions, mixing artificial materials in gold or silver with the fresh flowers seems permissible if so desired. Rarely do we get the chance of arranging flowers for a Diamond Wedding but large chunks of glass on a mirrored base with pure white flowers would admirably suit this sparkling occasion.

5

The Way Ahead

FREE-STYLE FLOWER ARRANGEMENT

It was not until the 1950s that a new modern style of arranging evolved and was accepted at flower shows in Britain. Since then there have been many shifts and changes although its foundations are still firmly based on all the accepted principles of good design. Sometimes known as 'free-style' or 'free-form' its characteristics are based upon economy of plant material and the emphasis on space within the design.

Modern homes with modern furnishings have undoubtedly influenced many people in their approach to arranging and they have found that clear-cut designs with bold plant material suit the modern environment better than the large mass arrangements of old. Added to this, it is a challenge to break away from tradition and strive for the unusual, and it is a stimulating and satisfying exercise to allow one's artistic individuality to be given rein.

For this style of arranging it is essential to have the right flowers or impact material, the right foliage or outline material and the right container—all are equally important. However, your source of inspiration may be from any of these. Sometimes it is a new container which is the catalyst, other times it may be an unusual branch formation or even an exquisite flower.

Containers

Rough or smooth textured containers in earthy colours and of geometric shapes are possibly the easiest to find and the advent of craft potters has made the search much easier.

See page 84
Copper piping was the inspiration for this design. Two pieces were each gently persuaded into an ellipse and the larger was carefully manipulated to give a gently curving indentation. Wooden dowelling was inserted into the piping at the ends so that the shape could be impaled on the pinholder. Two lilies arrest the eye in the shining framework.

See page 85
The trimmed iris leaves make a fascinating three-dimensional outline for this design. Two long reeds are bent at angles to further emphasize this pattern and the three orange lilies are carefully inserted to follow the outline. The modern green-glazed footed container has matching green stones to cover the mechanics.

Brightly coloured containers, too, should also be considered although they present a greater challenge in selecting the supporting items to get the right combination. The proportions of any container should be pleasing in itself otherwise it will never look right even when the flowers are added. Whilst an unusually-shaped pot would be a greater challenge it is often better to buy one of a more conventional shape which can be readily adapted to a variety of designs. Study the container and its possibilities well before your purchase. Many can have alternative uses by standing them on their sides or even upside down and these would make a better investment than one with a one-way-only use.

The flower arranger who is also a potter has a great advantage as pots can be specially designed to individual requirements. It is well worth attending day or evening classes in pottery if you get the opportunity as there is a certain thrill in arranging in your very own container. Pottery, of course, is not the only suitable medium—glass, acrylic, bamboo, metal as well as home-made containers all have their uses. In fact anything that will hold water or can be made to hold water can be used provided it has a 'modern' feel. Gimmicky props like bed springs, parts of motor cars or washing machines *et al* have no place in modern arranging except for giving it a bad name!

Outlines

Plant material of all descriptions, whether fresh, dried or preserved can be employed to make outlines. Inorganic objects, like acrylic shapes, metal strip and piping, rope and extruded plastic can also be considered for this purpose *provided they are aesthetically pleasing.*

● Suitable fresh plant material:

Tall sword-like leaves such as *Yucca, Phormium tenax* and iris are good examples. They can be inserted on to the pinholder at various angles when the points of the leaves can be trimmed flat or at 45 degrees to make dramatic outlines. They can also be made into loops of varying sizes by making a small snip in the leaf and threading the point through.

A fascinating billowing outline can be make from an *Aspidistra* leaf. This is done by slitting the length of either the left or right side of the main rib of the leaf at regular intervals with your thumbnail leaving a small margin at the edges. When this is done the leaf will open up like one of those expanding paper decorations seen at Christmas time and makes an interesting feature in an arrangement. These leaves can also be trimmed, rolled or looped.

Large palmate leaves from *Fatsia japonica* can be trimmed by taking off their points to make a more unusual shape. This can also be done with the fan palm (*Trachycarpus*) leaf.

Some large leaves like *Bergenia*, *Dracaena*, *Canna* and *Hosta* can be rolled and fastened at the base with an elastic band or staple to present another interesting shape.

Fresh green stems of reeds, grasses, *Cyperus* and *Scirpus* can be either bunched together, trimmed or bent at angles.

Some plant material can be manipulated, by training and tying into interesting shapes as it grows. Teasel, onion, leek and other *Alliums* lend themselves well to this type of treatment.

Other plant material such as broom, pussy willow, as well as weeping and corkscrew willow can easily be persuaded into interesting flowing curves with a little manipulation after cutting.

Any curved or angular branches can be trimmed to exaggerate their unusual shapes for outlines.

● Suitable dried plant material:

Nowadays there is a great variety of imported dried plant material to choose from and much of it is ideal for modern arrangements because of its bold form. It varies from large dried leaves of the various palms to fascinating seedheads like the curving 20in, 50cm *Poinciana* pods and the bleached fruit stems of the coconut palm. Flowers, too, are imported, like *Protea* and *Strelitzia*, but although they dry well they do not appear quite as exotic as when they are fresh.

Dried plant material of the bolder variety from the garden is always useful for outlines, like giant hogweed and *Angelica* stems which can easily be fashioned into a variety of shapes.

Ivy, vines and *Wisteria* provide stems of fascinating shapes. These can be easily stripped of their bark if they are peeled immediately they are cut. Failing this they will need to be soaked in a tank of water for a couple of days before stripping.

Strips of *Eucalyptus* and other tree barks all have their possibilities for making outlines.

Driftwood of all shapes and sizes makes some of the most spectacular silhouettes for modern designs. It can be left in its natural state or bleached, stained or even spray-painted depending on its use.

Burnt gorse or heather is another source of outline material if you don't mind getting your hands dirty.

See page 88
Fifteen separate pieces of buckthorn were cajoled into this curving, billowing sail shape. And because the natural silver colour was rather insipid they were sprayed black. The shining black triangular container integrates well into the design and three red gladioli are grouped together at the right for impact and to counter-balance the pull of buckthorn to the left.

See page 89
Stripped ivy is a wonderful medium for making outlines. In this design it is a compilation of three pieces glued together with the fourth piece inserted in the pinholder and brought forward to give extra depth. The shape itself will suggest where the most volume will be acceptable and that is where you should place the flowers.

The monkey puzzle tree (*Araucaria*) provides dramatic branches as does the *Salix* 'Setsuka' with its curved fasciated stems.

Bamboo from the garden can provide pattern-making material but the imported type with stems up to 2in, 5cm thick can be very spectacular and is worth seeking out. One possible source of supply is your local carpet shop. Thick bamboo is frequently used as a core to support rugs imported from the Far East.

Other organic materials for making original outlines, though not from the garden, are rattan and sea-wrack. Rattan can be purchased in many thicknesses and it is much easier to make permanent outlines with the thicker variety. This is easy to do. Soak the rattan in water (you will probably have to use the bath) until it is pliable. Bend and coil it into imaginative shapes, tie securely and then leave until completely dry. Because the dried rattan has a tendency to open out when untied the coils, spirals and shapes must be made much tighter than you really need. The thinner variety can effectively be looped loosely around other plant material for designing purposes.

Sea-wrack can be picked up around certain stretches of coastline—I have found it in Scotland and Northumberland. It is best to walk the tide-line and pick up pieces which have dried and already assumed wonderfully convoluted shapes naturally. But beware! When used in any arrangement sea-wrack must be given a false stem otherwise it will absorb water and flop as well as giving off a revolting smell!

● Suitable inorganic objects:

Any object in a suitable medium is well worth collecting for future use. Off-cuts of variously coloured acrylic and wrought-iron work can be integrated into arrangements and outlines can be fashioned from metal strip or piping. Polystyrene has its possibilities as well as waste extruded plastic in multivarious colours and shapes. In fact, all is grist to the mill where the flower arranger is concerned—but knowing what to keep and what to discard is something that cannot be taught—it is a matter of judgement.

Impact material

This is the material which gives the spark to your design. These are usually 'charismatic' flowers, those with an immediate attraction which catch and hold the eye. When visiting the florist for impact material, search for quality not quantity as just one or two of the more expensive flowers are effective.

Here are a few suggestions of garden or florist's flowers which make good eye-catchers:

Allium	*Kniphofia*
Amaryllis belladona	lilies (all types)
Anthurium	*Nerine*
Arum	*Orchid*
camellia	paeony
chrysanthemum	*Protea*
Clivia	roses (large flowered)
dahlia	*Strelitzia*
Gerbera	tulips (parrot & lily types)
hydrangea	*Vallota*

Sometimes smaller flowers can be grouped together to make a colour-block for greater impact.

You may also find that rosettes of leaves or even fruits can be employed as the highlight for your design.

Seedheads, too, can make unusual impact material. The larger kinds from *Alliums*, leeks, *Acanthus mollis*, artichoke and *Phormium tenax* are ideal used in ones or twos while the smaller seedheads like poppy and *Centaurea macrocephala* are best grouped together.

Now that we have discussed choice of container, outline material and impact material we need to know how to put them together to make a free-style design. While it is impossible to teach this style of arranging it is possible to suggest guidelines for channelling your ideas. In the final analysis it comes down to the individual's artistic sensibility and ability to create a design that is entirely original. Be inspired by others but do not copy. Be free-thinking and original and at the same time work within all the accepted principles of good design and you will find it a most stimulating challenge.

Guidelines
Free-style arranging is more akin to modern sculpture with its emphasis on line and space. Restraint is the key word and only

See page 92
This modern shining black container has two compartments for holding plant material and is a dramatic feature in itself. Four curlicues of black wisteria are threaded through each other like giant metal puzzles to form this arresting outline of enclosed spaces. Because of their equally unusual form and texture the two *Anthuriums* make ideal highlights for the design.

See page 93
Two long bamboo poles were the source of this original home-made container. They were cut into lengths of various sizes and constructed into this free-standing form for holding flowers. Segments of bamboo intended to hold water can be swirled round once or twice with polyurethane varnish to make them waterproof. Ivy and yellow lilies complete the picture.

that which is absolutely necessary is acceptable; further embellishment only detracts and obscures the main thrust of the design. Simplicity is what we are striving for but it is often difficult to attain—but therein lies part of the fascination of this challenging way of arranging. The secret is to achieve a delicate balance between all the component parts of the design so that it appears perfect in every particular.

Making a start—The best way to start is to plunge right in and then learn from your mistakes. Placing your first item in the container is probably the most difficult part. It is akin to putting your first brush strokes on a blank canvas or writing your first words on an empty page. It takes a certain amount of courage but once you start things have a way of moving forward and gaining momentum. Start by putting your first placement out of balance and then proceed by adding another to rectify the imbalance. Add a few more items, creating the design as you go along. Stand back and study it regularly and if you are not completely happy with the way things are going, start again. The more you practise the more skilled you will become in knowing where to put each item for the best effect. Sometimes the more dominant item will be at the top of your design which is contrary to the more traditional way of arranging. Nevertheless it will look right as a compensating item is inserted to restore the balance. Proportions, too, do not necessarily need to be conventional and can be exaggerated to obtain the effect you are striving for. The depth of the design is another important factor so material should be placed both forward and backward to emphasize the third dimension. Crossing lines also make us aware of space and again create depth. The use of enclosed space within the design is another factor to be considered. A small enclosed area has greater 'eye-pull' than a larger one and so it should be left empty for greater effect. On the other hand a larger area which is not as strong visually can be enhanced by the introduction of plant material.

Colour is yet another important factor and although we first think of vivid hues for this style of arranging, more subtle colours can also be used effectively. Texture, too, can play its part but here again restraint is needed.

A 'modern' flower arranger has to be a good technician and be able to devise ways of fastening plant material and other objects securely, seemingly without any visible means of support. If you are not able to do this satisfactorily, many of your designs will be ruined because you will have to hide the obtrusive mechanics with extra plant material. This is something else which comes with experience and you will eventually amaze yourself with your own ingenuity!

Theory is all very well but practical work is the only way to learn. These illustrations give examples of different ways of using plant material and other objects. A careful study of each will help you to analyse the way in which various aspects of the design have been put together and how specific effects have been achieved. They will also help you to see that many of the mundane objects we have around us can be presented in a completely different and exciting way lifting them from their utilitarian purpose into the realms of art.